Living Better

Lois Rosenthal

handwritten and illustrated by
Michael Streff

Writer's Digest Books
9933 Alliance Road, Cincinnati, Ohio 45242

Library of Congress Cataloging in Publication Data

Rosenthal, Lois
   Living better

   Includes index.
   1. Consumer education.   I. Title.
TX 335.R69   640.73   78-17233
ISBN 0-911654-59-3

For Richard Rosenthal
husband/fellow dreamer/publisher
With love and appreciation

Credits

A great many people—experts in fields as far ranging as managing cities to gathering wild food—gave their time and expertise to the preparation of Living Better. For their caring, kindness and unlimited generosity, I am grateful to: Gene Beaupre, Toni Birckhead, John Brennan, Linda Budai, Ricki Chrusciel, Sandy Clo, Pat di Lonardo, William Donaldson, Jack Farrell, Stephen Glassman, Gloria Haffer, Mike Haffer, Ted Herklotz, Jessica Lazarus, Barbara Marcus, Michael McKechnie, Richard Molby, Noel Morgan, Frederick Payne, Pat Phelan, Frances Jones Poetker, Joe Poetker, Vera Raupe, Patricia Roginski, Beverly Tonkens, Gerald Tonkens, James Vastine, Marge Warren, Leo Wayne, Janet Wesley, Betty Wood, George Young.

I am indebted to Kirk Polking, who not only edited Living Better, but also contributed a never-ending flow of ideas; and to Budge Wallis and Jeff Lapin who spread the word.

Table of Contents

Preface

All of us who live in the city have had our pressure gauges register to the point where we've wanted to get out, pitch a tent on top of a mountain, live off wild berries and never hear a phone ring for the rest of our lives. But few of us ever get past the daydream stage. We're plugged into our jobs, responsible to our families, obligated to our communities and, most times, in spite of the hassle, committed to our way of life.

And even though life in the city may have us reaching for more Alka Seltzer than we care to admit, it also provides us with limitless opportunities. All we have to do is see them. And <u>Living Better</u> shows you how to see. Something just that simple is the most important ingredient. It's a state of mind, a point of view, a way to observe what you look at every day just a little differently so that what you see takes on new meaning.

Junkyards are not just the end-of-the-line for twisted metal, they're full of treasures you can bring home and reuse. Weeds that grow along the side of the expressway can decorate your house, vocational school students can curl your hair or fix your car, Uncle Sam's castoffs are yours for the bidding, and if you want to vacation somewhere exotic, try trading homes with someone in another city.

Living Better points out these possibilities and more—uncovering simple alternatives.

Yes, there is a number to call to cut the red tape of the federal government. Yes, there is an answer to the overpackaging and waste we all have to pay for. Yes, there is something you can do about clothing that falls apart after one wearing. Instead of feeling frustrated and angry because "things don't work," _Living Better_ shows you how to get the system to work for you.

As urban life becomes more complicated, urban dwellers have to be more foxy. As prices rise, all of us have to be more savvy consumers. More creative. More aware of what is around us and how to put it to use. That's what _Living Better_ is all about.

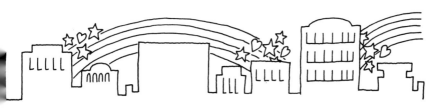

Recycle

Recycling is the creative use of those inevitable packaging throwaways that flow incessantly into our homes. Plastic bags from the produce department of the supermarket and the larger variety that encase your newspapers like sausages are just two examples. Rubber bands, Styrofoam meat trays, egg cartons, cereal boxes, coffee cans, cardboard rolls from the middle of paper towels and toilet paper, glass spice jars or tin ones, plastic liquid detergent squeeze bottles - what do you do with all of them? Well, you can simply pitch them or try to use as many as possible for a second purpose. I find the last alternative more appealing because recycling not only saves you money when you put all those packaging inventions to work, but also eliminates a ton of waste.

Number one nightmare - plastic bags. Do those we stick in kitchen drawers multiply while we are sleeping? When I pick out my own fruit in the supermarket and take care to pass up pre-packaged varieties to avoid waste, I wind up having to put my oranges and apples in plastic bags to get them weighed and priced. Two newspapers a day are delivered in plastic bags in rainy or snowy weather. Trying to use all of them can be a losing game. To start winning, stop buying boxes of plastic bags, and use

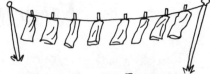

the ones you collect. Wash them,
turn them inside out to dry
and they can be used over
and over. Cut some
smaller to pack sandwiches for brown bag lunches. Freeze
food in them. Use them for stuffing pillows. Put your child's foot in
a plastic bag before you stick it into his galoshes. They go
on more easily and help keep his feet warm.

Plastic net bags, like the ones oranges
come in, can be hung on a hook over the bathtub
to hold tub toys.

If you want to get crafty with plastic
bags, you can braid them into a jump rope.

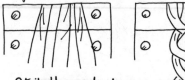
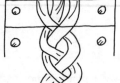

Stick the ends of
three bags into a drawer
to secure them and start braiding. Keep adding bags until you
have the length you want and
then tie the ends with yarn.

Plastic bag rugs are useful, too, in front of the
kitchen sink where the floor always takes a beating. Cut plastic
bags crosswise into double-strand strips and slipknot them
together until you have a long string of "yarn." With a crochet hook,

Recycle

chain a strip about 18 inches long and single crochet up one side of the chain and down the other. Add extra stitches on the ends to keep the rug from turning into a basket. Keep going until the rug is the size you want. To clean it, swish it in soapy water or hose it down.

Rubber bands? Squeeze some together and then start wrapping others around them to make a ball - any size you want. They're good bouncers, too. Chain rubber bands together to make a jump rope.

Wrap a few around a glass to keep it from slipping out of your child's hands.

Put a couple on the ends of wire hangers to keep your clothes from falling into a heap on the closet floor. No fair slipping rubber bands around doorknobs and pretending you don't see them!

Plastic ice cream containers can be used for storing or freezing food. Start seedlings in smaller ones. If you get the urge to rearrange your living room, put the legs of heavy furniture in plastic containers and everything will slide over the rugs more easily.

Styrofoam egg cartons are handy ice cube trays if you need extra for a party. Odd pieces of fruit or leftovers can be

3

frozen in them, too. Separate buttons, beads, odds and ends in cartons. Use them for a seedling nursery by placing half an eggshell inside each compartment. Fill the shell with loam, plant your seed, and, when it's ready to be transferred outside, plant the shell and the plant. The eggshell will decompose and enrich the soil.

Junk mail isn't junk if you use the backs of letters and envelopes for shopping lists or telephone messages. Answer notes on notes you receive and explain what you're doing with a stamp like this.

TO CONSERVE OUR
NATIONAL FORESTS—
THE REPLY TO YOUR
LETTER HAS BEEN
WRITTEN ON YOUR
LETTER.

You can buy one at any stationery store.

Coffee tins or any large tins are great organizers. Nail them to a wall to make bins. If you can get your hands on institutional-size cans, they're best for this.

Orange juice cans are favorites for pre-schoolers to decorate as pencil holders for parents. Any tin can can be sprayed, contact papered, slathered with string, noodles, stars, whatever. It all depends on how much time and creativity you want to invest. They do the very same thing if you leave them plain.

Glass baby food jars are perfect for storing nails and screws. If you make preserves or jam, use the jars you collect instead of buying new ones. Big glass jars (institutional-size, again, are terrific) can hold flour, sugar, tea or any condiment you keep on your kitchen counter.

Save the plastic lids that come with some tin cans for separators when you freeze hamburger patties.

An empty soft drink carton can be a carryall for cleaning compounds as you work your way from room to room. Stash it under the sink or in a closet to keep everything together for fast grabbing when you need it.

Large detergent boxes can hold special magazines you want to save and keep together. Cut them like this and you're all set.

A chipped dish on top of a bowl in the refrigerator saves you from going the plastic wrap route to keep food fresh. Grandma was pretty foxy.

Living Better

Holey pantyhose can stuff pillows or be cut in strips to tie plants if you're a gardener. Since nylon stretches, it won't strangle your tomato plants when you tie them to the stake. Worn-out pillow cases can be converted into clothes bags. Just make a hole in one end and slip it over a hangar.

Cut up bedraggled fake fur coats and make them into pillows or throw rugs for children's rooms.

Save thread, yarn and string pieces inside a mesh bag, then hang it on a branch in spring to give the birds a nest-building boost. Stuff a tee shirt and use it as a pillow. Pass a big tee shirt on to a littler kid to use as a night shirt.

Newspaper and brown paper bags are fine for wrapping packages. Directions for using all kinds of paper are found in the Giving Chapter. If you wish, you can cut brown paper bags into strips and weave them into placemats.

Cut a dozen strips about 3½ inches wide and about 15 inches long. Twelve more strips should be a couple of inches longer.

Fold the strips lengthwise, and then

Recycle

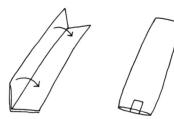

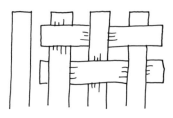

fold them again, being sure that all the cut edges meet along the center fold. Use masking tape to hold one short end of each strip together.

Line up the shorter strips close together and weave the longer ones over and under these, alternating the order every other strip.

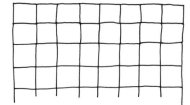

Push the strips firmly together after each row. When you are finished, glue all the ends under. Spray with a clear finish.

Newspaper crafts are endless, too. Here are a couple of easy examples.

Apron

Fold paper in half and cut an arc from the side to the top.

Open and place string or yarn through the holes. Tape over the holes to keep from tearing.

Dustpan

Fold edges inward about 2 inches.

Bring up bottom edge and fold in half. Turn in sides and staple closed.

Roll the top down
and staple the
layers from inside.
For a sharp edge,
trim it with tape.

A whole world of children's toys can be created with zillions of unsuspecting objects you have at home. Tune up your own orchestra. Make a flute out of a paper tube by punching holes in it about an inch apart. Cover one end with waxed paper and hum or sing into it. Tie four heavy nails to a stick with string. Strike the nails with a dull knife and you'll hear bell-like sounds. Cut a hole in the top of a shoe box and stretch five rubber bands across it lengthwise. There's your banjo. Fill yogurt cups, tin cans, medicine bottles or margarine tubs with uncooked rice, dried beans, stones or buttons. Who needs maracas? To make a tambourine, glue two paper plates together and punch holes around the edges. Also punch holes in some bottle caps with a hammer and nail, and tie two caps to each hole in the plate with a string. Put Kleenex over a comb and hum. Enough noise?

Make stilt walkers from cans. Little kids can start with tuna cans until they are ready to tackle taller ones. Remove

Recycle

a lid, and punch two holes in the bottom of each can directly opposite each other about ½ inch from the edges. Put a strong string through the holes and tie a knot inside to secure it. Slip your elbows through the looped string and you're in business.

Plastic soap bottles are great bathtub squirt toys. Clorox bottles turn into piggy banks with a few simple additions. Old socks are fine hand puppets. Or use them for the head of a hobby horse. Just stuff a sock, insert a broomstick all the way into the heel and tie it on tightly. Decorate with a face and mane.

Leaky rubber gloves? Cut off the fingers for - you guessed it - finger puppets. Mount greeting cards, valentines or Christmas cards on cardboard. Cut them out in irregular patterns for do-it-yourself puzzles. Punch a series of holes in cards and use them for sewing. Mismatched shoestrings can be your thread. You can do all these same things with magazine scenes. Or cut out words from magazines and paste them on paper to form a message for let's-pretend-telegrams.

String buttons or pasta instead of store-bought beads. Make building blocks from milk cartons (just cut them the size you wish and tape down the edges), soap boxes, Jell-o boxes,

9

round rolled oats containers. These same containers can be anything you or your child imagines.

Stand milk cartons like bowling pins, and, well, you take it from there.

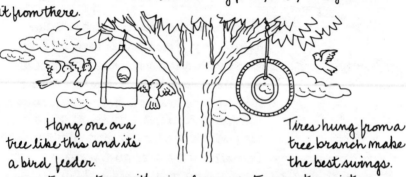

Hang one on a tree like this and it's a bird feeder.

Tires hung from a tree branch make the best swings.

Egg cartons with pipe cleaner antennae turn into caterpillars. A truck tire laid flat on the ground with sand dumped inside turns into a sandbox. If you're a city dweller without a yard, make an indoor sandbox from an old plastic dishpan. Just make sure you spread newspaper or dry cleaning bags underneath to cut your cleanup time to a minimum. Brown bags, again, can make masks or whole costumes depending on the size bag you put on the size kid.

It really is endless. This chapter doesn't pretend to be the end-all of craft ideas, but it is just a sampling of some of the simple things you can do to reclaim recyclables. More ideas are scattered throughout this book in the Clothing, Food, Giving, Used and Abused chapters. For even more, check in at your local

Recycle

library and look up handcrafts in the card catalogue. You'll find drawersful of books as diverse as those dealing exclusively with newspaper crafts to others which give directions for cupcake container creations.

If you still have leftovers, separate into boxes what your community recycling center will accept. Many cities have added places where you can bring cans, glass bottles, newspapers, cardboard, magazines and more. They like it best if you take the lids off cans and flatten them before you bring them in. It's also easier to store them at home this way, too. The money made from selling cans and bottles often goes to further environmental education projects, so it's all worthwhile.

If you want to make extra money from what you save, sell your newspaper, magazines, cardboard and other waste paper to waste paper dealers. Look in the Yellow Pages of your phone directory under "Waste Paper" and you will find dealers listed. Call and see what they will accept. Think about your club or school group having a money-raising paper drive. Many dealers will bring Dumpsters to any site you specify for group members to deliver paper. Just set up the drop-off date in advance and the dealer will come and haul everything away.

Look under "Scrap Metals" in the Yellow Pages for dealers who will take your tin or aluminum cans.

Kids can clean up ballfields and playfields where abandoned pop cans flourish. If you provide the transportation to the scrap yard, kids can turn their cleanup efforts into extra money. It gives the environment a face-lift at the same time. Ask what other kinds of metals these dealers will accept and look around the house for what else you can get rid of. Don't forget about worn-out car batteries. They'll take those for sure.

Composting

Recycling food leftovers into meals will be covered in the Food chapter, but for down-and-out food throwaways, think about creating a compost pile in your backyard. You will not only be getting rid of garbage, you will also be creating rich mulch to use around your bushes, flowers and trees. If you have a large wooded yard, it's perfect for composting, but there are also ways a small city lot can be utilized.

Pile materials to be composted in a heap or a bin-type structure if you want to obstruct it from view and keep it tidy (better for a smaller yard with other houses close by). Bins are usually 4 to 6 feet high, 3 to 5 feet wide, any convenient length, and made of

Recycle

wire fencing, open brick work or boards. Collect your grass clippings or fall leaves to start the pile, then add food scraps and cover them over with the leaves or clippings. The general rule is that everything that has lived once will rot down in a compost heap, so anything that isn't synthetic can be composted. Bones take an awfully long time, though, so I avoid them.

You can be very scientific about composting and layer organic materials with any kind of garden fertilizer that is high in nitrogen. (Buy it at any garden store or nursery.) The whole idea is to get bacteria working so the compost will break down. Fertilizer heats it up faster, which will make it rot more quickly than if you let it alone, and also adds extra nutrients. If you turn compost periodically, it helps the breaking down process as does keeping it damp. But if your heap is in the shade, the moisture will be taken care of naturally. Finally, the bottom of the heap should be on the ground to give the earthworms a chance to tunnel up and aerate the whole lot.

I begin a compost pile in the fall with piles of dried leaves from the yard. We keep a plastic bag in the kitchen sink for throwaway food scraps and then carry it out to the compost pile when it's full. After dumping the food, whoever carries it out kicks leaves over it. This method is completely unscientific, but we always come up with good mulch

ready to be used in the yard by spring. However, if you haven't used anything to enrich or help break down the compost, throw a few handfuls of high-nitrogen fertilizer in every wheelbarrow load you use to make a nutritious mixture. Compost alone rarely provides enough nutrients for your plants. And it has to be in a thoroughly inorganic state (completely broken down) before it has a positive effect. Ideally, it should be a rich, dark brown.

One detriment to composting is that it can draw rats. Since my pile is in the woods far enough from our house, I don't worry about it. Besides, raccoons, possums and all kinds of critters have a fine spread all winter long.

One of the best compost sights I ever saw when I went out to make a new food deposit was a box turtle munching contentedly away on an aging slice of tomato vinaigrette. Bon Appétit! But if you feel your compost pile would draw the rat population of America to your door, you may have to abandon the compost idea.

Recycle

For further specific, wonderfully detailed information about composting, call your county agent at the Department of Agriculture Extension Service listed under the U.S. Government in your phone directory. He'll answer your questions on the phone or send free brochures containing pictures and instructions. (More about services county agents provide in the Using the Feds chapter.)

Another source of mulch is right under your nose. All the companies that clear lines for gas and electric and telephone companies will give you ground-up tree limbs they take down - free. Call the utility and ask for the head of the department in charge of clearing lines. He will usually put your name on a waiting list and have the mulch delivered to you when crews are working in your area. Wood mulch has to rot before it's usable. High-nitrogen fertilizer can be added to help this happen, or add it after the wood shavings decompose naturally to enrich it.

Another word on wood mulch. If you want it - you're going to have to accept an entire truckload. If you have gerbils or guinea pigs to house, it helps in using it up. Make garden

paths or patio areas. Share with a friend.

Look, it's easier to throw out tin cans than wash them, take off the lids, stomp on them and store them. And I'm not crazy about the time it takes to lug boxes of them to the recycling center. But at the same time I complain about it,

Living Better

I also feel good knowing that what I have used can be used again. The whole recycling issue is one you have to decide for yourself. But there is something that you can do that is no trouble at all and won't take a moment from your day. Avoid waste by refusing packaging you don't want in the first place.

Carry a basket or collapsible string bag if you have lots of errands to do. If not, you'll wind up with stacks of little bags from each store. Take your extra brown bags back to the supermarket when you go shopping and have your groceries packed in them. The supermarkets will love you because you're saving them money. While the love affair lasts, ask that the savings be passed back to you.

And, talking about passing along savings, don't forget:

OLD BREAD IS FOR THE BIRDS!!

Weeds

Next time you hit the expressway, look for the cone-shaped nettles that seem to flourish along the side of the road. If you can pull over on the shoulder without causing a major collision, gather a bundle and bring them home. Fill an old umbrella stand or any long skinny container with the nettles and place it in a bare spot in your house. You can fill whole corners of rooms with a few containersful. My favorites are red clay sewer tiles of varying heights bought from any building supply yard. Not only is their shape exactly right, but the clay and the weeds make a happy marriage.

This is one example of how you can use wild things that grow in the most unlikely places to beautify your home. Vacant lots, cracks in the sidewalk all produce weeds and flowers you've probably passed a hundred times and never noticed because they're always there. Start noticing! If you can get to the woods or an open field, it's easy to find armloads of treasures. Take a drive out to the country and then take a walk. If you live in the suburbs, stroll around the block and really look around you.

NETTLES
AHEAD
NEXT 2 EXITS

17

Gathering

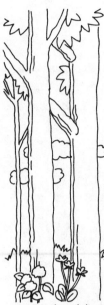

The art of gathering wild flowers, weeds, seeds, pods, and branches can be as scientific as you want it to be or as informal as a walk in the woods. There are tons of books written on the subject, containing intricate instructions on gathering and drying methods you may want to consult. I have listed several at the end of this section. My general procedure is rather unorthodox. When I take walks and spot interesting growing things, I either bring them home and put them in water or hang them upside down to dry. The worst thing that can happen is I wind up with flower petals scattered all over the floor. But, there are some basic guidelines that will help your searches be successful ones.

First, you may want to buy a book to help you identify what you find. Roger Tory Peterson and Margaret McKenny's <u>Field Guide to Wildflowers</u> (Houghton Mifflin, $5.95, paperback) is an encyclopedic volume with excellent drawings you can find at any bookstore. You don't have to use a guide, however. I rarely know the names of what I bring home, but it is a help. There is one rule everyone should observe

Weeds

when gathering wildflowers. Do not take everything from one single spot. Pick a little here and there and never harvest an entire area. If there's only one flower growing, leave it alone. And be careful not to pull anything up by the roots. Judicious harvesting stimulates flower growth because, when blooms are left to die and dry on the plant, bloom production of that plant is usually low. Picking stimulates new growth, but temperance is the key.

Also, what we consider weeds is food for wild animals and birds, so the idea is to share the wealth. Some plants, on the protected list, are in danger of extinction, so you don't want to pick those. To find out which plants in your area you should leave alone, write to the Wildflower Preservation Society, 3740 Oliver St., N.W., Washington, D.C. 20015.

One last word. Better ask permission to pick on private property that doesn't happen to be yours. Park property, too.

The best time to gather wildflowers, if you want to use them in live arrangements, is in the early morning or late afternoon when the day is coolest and the plants are most turgid. Since a large percentage of a plant is water, from the moment you pick it, you should try to prevent as much water loss as possible. Put flowers in a plastic bag and keep it sealed as you gather. The air in the bag, when you open and close it to accept new additions,

19

combined with the condensation from the moisture of the plants, will keep them in good condition. Wrapping stems of plants in dampened newspaper before putting them in bags also helps. And always try to keep cut flowers out of direct sunlight.

To pick flowers for dried arrangements, take your walk during the heat of the day when plants contain the least amount of moisture. But be sure you do not pick wilted flowers because they will not preserve well. For drying, plants should always be at the peak of their perfection. If you're after foliage, leaves should have good color and be unspotted, as well as firm and dry.

Preserving

Many flowers and weeds simply dry by themselves at the end of the season like the nettles, and, in that case, you can bring them home for instant arrangements without any bother. Pods, seeds, grasses and grains, too. But if the flowers need drying, there are several methods to choose from.

Easiest is air drying. Some flowers and foliage can be placed directly in a vase without water and will dry perfectly well upright. Common examples you can use this method with are pussy willows, wild grasses, grains and flowers with large composite heads and sturdy stalks, such as Queen Anne's lace and cockscomb. Most have to be hung upside down in small bunches in a dry, dark place for a few weeks before they are ready to be

Weeds

used. A simple invention that takes up little space is to hang branches from strings of different lengths on coat hangers. This will allow good air circulation around drying materials. Most everlastings air dry well this way, as do baby's breath, goldenrod, yarrow and artemesia to name a few common ones. But don't be afraid to experiment with other kinds. Also, if you want to keep flowers dust-free, cover them with plastic bags punched with holes to let the air through. When the flowers are thoroughly dried, spray them with a clear matte varnish to keep them from shedding, to keep insects away and to protect them from moisture. I use hairspray and it does the trick.

Flowers can also be dried chemically, and this method usually preserves their color best. Silica gel is a popular drying agent which you can buy at craft stores, flower shops and some hardware stores. It is also reusable.

①

Pour silica gel about one inch deep in a shoe box, tin or plastic container.

②

Place the plants (flowers should have stems cut to one inch in length) stem first in the material so the petals are resting in the chemical substance.

③

Then sprinkle silica gel around and over the flowers in a thin layer – just enough to cover them.

Put a lid on the box and seal it tightly with tape. Drying time depends on the fleshiness of the plant - the thicker it is, the longer it takes.

Sand may also be used as a drying agent, but it must be completely dry first. Either expose it to hot sunlight or pour it on cookie tins and heat it in a low oven for a few hours. Let the sand cool before you use it to dry flowers, in the same way you used silica gel, except the box should be left uncovered.

A combination of equal parts Borax and cornmeal plus six tablespoons of salt can also be used as a drying agent. So can detergents that are labeled high in enzymes.

When you are ready to arrange chemically dried flowers, tape florist's wire next to the one-inch stems and continue taping the entire length of the wire to disguise it. Green florist's tape is the best to use. To finish the process, spray flowers with lacquer to protect them from moisture.

To preserve branches of leaves, crush the bottom two inches with a hammer so the fiber and bark split, mix equal parts glycerine and water and place the branches in the liquid. (Some experts recommend one-part glycerine to two-parts water and that the water should

Weeds

be boiled and mixed while it is hot.) During the few weeks it takes to process the branches, occasionally wipe the leaves with a cloth dampened with the solution. Magnolia, eucalyptus, beech and evergreens turn out beautifully, but, to insure success, make sure branches are cut before leaves reach the point of abscission. This means cut branches before late August, when the leaves are still green and the tree has not yet cut off liquid to the leaf causing it to change color, dry up and drop. If the branches aren't prime, you won't be happy with the results.

Leaf pressing is an old art. Autumn, when colors are vivid, is the favorite time of most collectors. Pick freshly fallen leaves and place them between several layers of newspaper, making sure the leaves do not touch each other. Cover them with heavy books and as the leaves are being pressed, the newspaper will absorb their moisture. If you remove them before they are completely dry, leaf edges will curl.

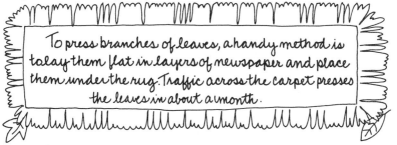

To press branches of leaves, a handy method is to lay them flat in layers of newspaper and place them under the rug. Traffic across the carpet presses the leaves in about a month.

You can also press the leaves with a warm iron. Place a

leaf between two pieces of wax paper; cover with newspaper and press. The wax from the paper will melt and coat the leaf to preserve it. When the leaf cools, press it overnight between the pages of a book.

Treasures that need no processing can be found most anywhere.

Look for buckeyes, burrs, acorns, pine cones; all varieties of nuts and seeds, pods, bird's nests, feathers and broken eggs if they are on the ground; pieces of weathered wood and bark; honeycombs; lichens; interesting rocks; dried up insects like cicadas, dragonflies, butterflies; shed snake skins, and, if you are lucky enough to live by the sea - glorious shells.

Look for mushrooms in cool, moist areas that do not get direct sunlight. They seem to pop up after a good rain. If you don't dry them right after you pick them they will spoil quickly. So if you find them on a bright day, wrap string around the stems and hang them upside down tied to a clothes hanger in the sun. They will dry in about an hour. Or dry them with silica gel. Using either method, you have more good things to add to your collection.

Arranging

A basket of pine cones in front of a fireplace is always lovely. (If the pine cones you gather are closed, heat them on a cookie tin in a low oven until they open.) Baskets of shells on a low table bring back memories of a trip to the ocean. Or show them off to better advantage in a glass cannister. Arrange lichens on an interesting piece of wood. A single rock perched on a stand, milkweed pods in a flat dish—perfect.

Pick milkweed pods when they're green, scoop out the insides, stuff them with Kleenex to keep them open while they dry a silvery yellow. You can let them open by themselves but first stick them inside a plastic bag.

Osage oranges are fragrant fall finds. I pile them in baskets—which I seem to do with many things I find—and enjoy them until they are too rotten to hang on to. To preserve them, slice them in half as you would an orange and heat them in a low oven. They retain their color, although some curl and make marvelous radial flower forms.

Layer seeds and nuts in apothecary jars. Collect airline liquor bottles for miniature dried grass arrangements. Use a plastic medicine vial filled with one fresh flower to poke into dried arrangements for added color.

When I talk about making flower arrangements, I don't mean formal florist-like works of art. If you are able to do this, you're way ahead. To make up for my limited arranging abilities, I rely on interesting containers to just, well, put things in. As I said before, baskets are my old faithfuls. Containers with small openings like jugs do the arranging for you. Tall, skinny things like the sewer tiles, umbrella stands, even an old copper fire extinguisher I found, make arranging tall weeds a cinch. Cups and saucers, creamers, teapots, vases you can pick up for a few cents at thrift shops are fine for smaller things.

Another aspect of "arranging" is to go ahead and mix objects that are unlikely companions. Frances Jones Poetker, one of the authors of Wild Wealth, is an acclaimed authority on the creative use of all growing things. An afternoon spent with her yielded these combinations that complement each other because of shape and color: a bowl full of russet pears, acorns and brown nuts; osage oranges piled in a large bowl with a few red cabbages or Bermuda onions for added color; feathers, even if they are from a poor old starling, mixed with leaves in a vase; thorns from honey locust branches with flowers stuck on the ends, or even kumquats.

This brings in the whole issue of using fruits and vegetables creatively. For those of us who can't get to a woods, we can easily make it to our neighborhood supermarket, which always yields a bumper crop of materials to use.

Italian onions, in a basket, were the perfect centerpiece at a party when I served lasagna. I stuck daisies between the onions to liven them up. Pomegranates (dried, they turn a deep Sienna red and last for years) are fine in bowls. Fill tiny clay flower pots with small heads of Bibb lettuce in rows down the middle of the table to create a miniature lettuce patch. Flower pots filled with parsley work just as well. Stick a wood or ceramic animal on a flat dish with parsley piled around

it to create a jungle. A pineapple top can be as versatile as you please. If you have an animal planter with an opening in its back, stick the pineapple top in it. I put a pineapple top in a plain little sugar bowl and stuck feathers in the leaves. If you are having lots of guests and lots of pineapple for dessert, stick a pineapple top in a container at each place. Carrot tops in water are fine. So are the tops of beets. Buy bunches of celery and tie each one with a pale blue or green velvet ribbon. Pile them in rows, four on the bottom, three in the next row, then two, then one for a celery pyramid in the middle of your table. Buy fresh artichokes and stuff each petal with Kleenex so they will dry open - like flowers. This will take about a week. Then - you guessed it - put them in a basket. Crisp red apples in a bowl are a simple and easy complement to the middle of your dining room table or a table in your living room. Try oranges. Lemons. Any combination of fruit as a centerpiece can double as a dessert.

You can dry vegetables, too, just like weeds and flowers. Hang them upside down in bunches. Hot peppers threaded on a long string are a beautiful kitchen decoration while they're drying. Experiment with artichokes, garlic, broccoli, brussel sprouts, onions - even cauliflower or cabbage. At Christmas you can attach these dried vegetables to a ring of florist's wire to create a wreath. Garnish with dried herbs or other dried staples you've collected.

Weeds

Gourds turn up at supermarkets in the fall. Use them for a month or so in an arrangement and then put them someplace warm and dry - to dry. They become very light and fade to muted beiges in the aging process. We should all look so good when we grow old.

Indian corn pops up at this time of year, too.

There are absolutely no rules for decorative dinner arrangements. Look around your house and use what you have handy. I have two favorite bird decoys that I rely on. Sometimes I use them with some birds' nests I found on the ground after a storm. Other times I take potted plants from window sills and put them on the table with the birds peeking out from under the ivy vines. I drag out a Swedish straw goat every

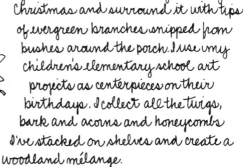

Christmas and surround it with tips of evergreen branches snipped from bushes around the porch. I use my children's elementary school art projects as centerpieces on their birthdays. I collect all the twigs, bark and acorns and honeycombs I've stacked on shelves and create a woodland mélange.

Frances Jones Poetker places three different vases of complementary shapes in the middle of the table and fills only one. This is the art of understatement. Or she arranges three lumps of coal in the center with one perfect white gardenia. For her, laminated egg cartons become centerpiece flower holders. She rings statues or small sculptures with wild asters or ivy. Gone-to-seed dried grass is stuck in the holes of salt shakers and dandelion stems are split in half vertically (they will curl up instantly) and balanced on the edge of a glass. Three toothpicks are tied together to make a tripod to hold half an eggshell. Fill the shell with water as a vase for flowers, celery tops, broccoli, Queen Anne's lace.

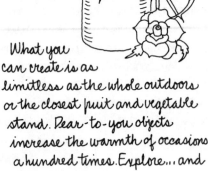

What you can create is as limitless as the whole outdoors or the closest fruit and vegetable stand. Dear-to-you objects increase the warmth of occasions a hundred times. Explore... and experiment.

How to Dry Flowers The Easy Way
Audrey Steiner Bugbee
Houghton Mifflin

The Arco Book of Dried and Pressed Flowers
Jean Derbyshire & Renee Burgess
Arco Publishing Co., Inc.

Wild Wealth
Paul Bigelow Sears, Marion
Rombauer Becker, Frances
Jones Poetker, Janice
Robert Forberg.
Bobbs-Merrill

Nature Crafts

Nature crafts is a world unto itself and one I face with a great deal of ambivalence. To paint a face on a rock seems a shame when the rock in its natural state has so much beauty. I would rather see a basket of pine cones than a sea of staring pine cone owls and a dish of acorns rather than an army of little men wearing hats. To me, beautiful nature craft objects are ones which retain the integrity of the materials used.

For instance, a plain old-fashioned nosegay of dried flowers framed with some odd bits of lace—a true love gift to anyone. Sachets are collections of all the sweet-smelling things you can find. Fill them with crumbled herbs you air dried. You can even dry herbs on a cookie sheet on the lowest possible setting of your oven. You can fill sachets with any appealing aroma—roses, lavender, mint geranium, rosemary, cloves, tarragon, marjoram. Dried orange, lemon and grapefruit peel create another kind of fragrance you can use. Just add a fixative (orris root is good and available where herbs and spices are sold) to any mix to make sure your fragrance lasts. Then place the mixture in a jar and seal the lid with masking tape and let it age for a few weeks in a cool dark place. During this period stir the mixture occasionally and reseal.

To make a sachet, you can simply spread an old fancy handkerchief scavenged from a thrift store on a table, pour your mixture in the center, gather the edges together, and tie them with a ribbon. If you can sew, make a shape you like and stuff it. Another sachet filler you can use is dried pine needles (balsam is wonderful). Just break the needles to release the scent. It's like giving someone a walk in the woods.

Barbara Marcus, a California crafts artist, makes "dream pillows" from the herbs and flowers she grows and the cloth scraps left over from her sewing projects. "My technique," she says, "derives directly from the Seminole Indians' traditional patterns."

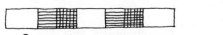

Sew a long stripe design— any combination of colors and lengths—and then cut that stripe at regular vertical intervals.

Rejoin it to make a new pattern.

You can also cut the original stripe on the bias, which produces other designs.

The square you create becomes the center of a pillow.

Weeds

Sew other strips around it and join to the back, leaving an opening to pour your herb/flower mix. Give it to someone as a bed throw. Sweet dreams!

A pomander is another love gift. Great closet sweeteners for kids to make grandmas at Christmas. Select a firm, fresh apple, orange or lime and make random holes in it with a sharp skewer. Insert cloves in the holes you've made. When the fruit is completely covered with cloves, roll it in a mixture of equal parts orrisroot or arrowroot and ground cinnamon. Wrap it in tissue paper or cheese cloth and hang it in a warm, dry place to age. As the fruit dries (it takes about three weeks), it will shrink and no part of the skin will show. Tie the pomander ball with a ribbon, bringing the ends together in a bow at the top. It's ready to be hung from a cord in a closet.

Spoon gourds can be made into bird feeders. Cut a hole in the center of the gourd and then fill it with bird seed. Drill a hole in the top and insert a wire or cord which is knotted inside. Tie the other end of the string to a tree. Larger gourds can be cut into bowls. Fill them with popcorn or nuts or with other dried materials. Small ones can be sugar spoons or flour scoops.

Living Better

A pine cone covered with peanut butter and rolled in bird seed is also a fine bird feeder. It's so simple.

Make a daisy chain – and wear it. Or use clover. Carrots cut in slices, strung, then dried for ten days in a warm place make fine ready-to-wear jewelry kids can do.

String cranberries or popcorn to decorate your Christmas tree. Float walnut shell halves with a candle stuck inside in a bowl of punch for kids' birthdays. Make an all-occasion tree from a dead branch which has been stuck in a container filled with plaster of Paris mixed with water. Wait a few minutes for the plaster mix to set before you insert the branch. Hang stars from it, pine cones, gumdrops, lollipops, Christmas ornaments, Halloween witches, felt hearts – anything.

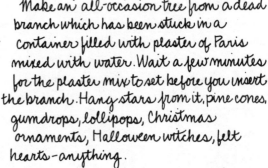

Branches can also be used as mobile suspenders for all the natural objects you've collected. String seashells from them to create wind chimes.

Start a sweet potato plant by pushing four or more

Weeds

toothpicks halfway into the bottom third of it. Place it in a full glass of water with the toothpicks resting on the top rim. Put it on a windowsill where it will get light and watch it sprout.

Make the most thoughtful notecards ever by pressing flowers and weeds between sheets of drawing or blotting paper and placing them underneath a heavy stack of books. You can sandwich lots of flowers and press many at one time by alternating layers of cardboard with the blotting paper. It may take about two weeks for the moisture of the flowers to be absorbed. When they are ready, carefully glue them to the front of plain notecards you have bought or made from construction paper.

The burrs that stuck on your clothes when you went weed collecting can now be stuck together to make a basket - in minutes. Use it as a container for small dried flowers or seeds.

Another supermarket pleasure - vegetables for printing. Bring home artichokes, apples, oranges, pears, onions - try them all. Place some padding (newspapers or napkins) under the paper you wish to print, and then brush tempera paint or printing ink on the cut side of the fruit or vegetable. Press it firmly on the paper and lift carefully to avoid smudging. Make random or pattern designs.

Try printing with leaves. Use fabric instead of paper. Let the print dry for 24 hours and then place the fabric on an ironing board. Cover it with newspaper and heat with an iron for a few minutes. Always wash the fabric by hand in warm water.

Zero in on a potato. Carve hearts, flowers, diamonds, initials and print with it using the very same method given above.

There are thousands more ideas. Where to find them? At your local library. Look in the card catalogue under nature, handcrafts and wildflowers.

Wild Foods

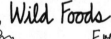

Ever think of eating the wild things you find instead of arranging them in vases? You can, only you have to be extremely careful. Identification, this time, is all important. The prime rule is, if you can't identify it, don't eat it. Even if you're 90% sure it is what you think it is, don't try it unless you're 100% positive.

Weeds

Hemlock closely resembles wild carrots. These are two weeds you certainly don't want to confuse. Also be careful to gather weeds in unsprayed areas. Pesticides are another substance you don't want to ingest. Ask, if you're not sure whether an area has been sprayed. But then, you really don't have to travel very far to gather wild food to eat. Salads are as close as the dandelions on your front lawn. Their young leaves are delicious. Crabapple jelly, steamed cattail stalks, watercress soup, wild strawberry sherbet—these can all become part of your daily fare if you are game to try them. It's also a good idea to be able to identify edible plants in case you ever become wilderness stranded.

All this is really nothing new. Man first lived on wild berries and plants since cultivation didn't start until centuries later.

Many city park naturalists teach courses in wild food collecting, so call your park board and see if they offer one. If not, and you want to try it on your own, here are some books that will help you identify and cook what you find.

Living Better

A Field Guide to Edible Wild Plants
of Eastern and Central North America
Lee Peterson
Houghton Mifflin

Deadly Harvest - A Guide To
Common Poisonous Plants
John M. Kingsbury
Holt, Rinehart and Winston

The Wild Gourmet
Babette Brackett and Maryann Lash
Godine

Stalking the Good Life
Euell Gibbons
David McKay Co.

Working With Nature, A
Practical Guide
John W. Brainerd
Oxford University Press

Eat The Weeds
Ben Charles Harris
self-published

A Naturalist's Guide to
Cooking With Wild Plants
Connie and Arnold Krochmal
Quadrangle - The New York
Times Book Co.

Edible Wild Plants
Oliver P. Medgser
Macmillan Co.

The Landscape We See
Garrett Eckbo
McGraw-Hill

The Edible Wild
B. Berglund and C.E. Bolsey
Scribner's

Human Poisoning from
Native and Cultivated Plants
James W. Hardin and
Jay M. Arena
Duke University Press

Used and Abused

Salvaging, scavenging, finding treasures in trash, junking—that's the fine art of getting something wonderful for nothing (legally) by simply staking claim to other people's throwaways. And people throw away incredible things, from large pieces of furniture to art treasures.

Someone purging an attic may stack some battered and worthless (to them) chairs and a table next to the garbage cans on the curb on pickup day. If you see them before the waste collectors do—they're yours. But don't drive around the block to think about whether you want them or not, because chances are, when you return, the table and chairs will have been stashed in another junker's car. That's a cardinal rule of junking.

Junking can be done on a casual basis by just retrieving something from the garbage when you happen to see it, or by careful planning. Dedicated junkers know the garbage pickup schedules of every prime neighborhood. These are easily obtained by calling your city's department of waste collection. The trick is to simply beat the trucks to the treasure. Some junkers favor late night picking

39

while others hit the cans in the early morning hours. Whatever time you choose, don't be amazed if you run into your tennis game gathered round the garbage.

Secondhand Stores

If you've missed out on junking freebies, you can still do well at secondhand furniture stores. Look in the Yellow Pages under "Furniture, Bought and Sold", and there will be lists of used furniture stores as well as auction houses and moving and storage companies. All of these places have store rooms packed with unlimited possibilities. Just realize that you'll likely see last years TV tables stacked next to a heap of tired mattresses, some cherry-laminated cardboard dressers and a few standard hopeless washing machines. But stuck in a corner can be just the pair of 30's kitchen chairs you've been looking for. Secondhand stores are definitely not antique shops and you're going to have to dig through mountains of monstrosities to get to the goodies - if there

are any. You may have to make the rounds many times before you find anything you consider worthwhile.

Many secondhand store owners pile up used furniture and sell it as "used furniture" whether it's fifty or five years old. Some know right well what the treasures are and charge accordingly. Pick ratty-looking places in neighborhoods to match. Those are where the best buys are. (Take a friend - a big one - with you.) I've found old Coke signs (50¢), fine wicker funeral baskets (25¢), Art Deco vases ($1), 30's wooden kitchen chairs (three for $11) and even some great quilts that were being used to wrap around furniture when it was loaded and unloaded on the trucks. Keep your sense of humor, have patience, and you're bound to hit pay dirt.

Junkyards

Wrecking company yards used to contain carved wooden bannisters and doors, stained glass windows, brass hardware - all the beautiful accessories which were saved by the wreckers before the house or building was demolished. Not these days. Hand

Living Better

wrecking is a thing of the past. If you see something that you want on a house to be torn down, contact the owner of the place and ask to buy it (chances are a dealer will have beat you to it), because once the wreckers go in with their heavy machinery, nothing is saved and nothing is left.

Some hope lies with small wrecking companies which will, at times, salvage pieces. I have found a few yards stacked with doors, windows, toilets, wash basins, used bricks, once even a pretty nice mantel and some wooden shutters. Windows can be used to create hotbeds in your garden, doors turn into coffee tables, desks or dining tables balanced on wooden horses or whatever other base you may want to use. I found stacks of slate tile at one place (nice for a front hall) and some huge stone gargoyles taken from the roof of a public library that for the life of me, I couldn't figure out what to do with.

Scrap metal yards (listed under "Scrap Metal" in the Yellow Pages) are also good places to scout. Giant companies may not want you around because they're afraid you may get in the way of one of their huge mashers or slicers. Just entering one of these

Used and Abused

places, because of the insurance risks, you're supposed to wear hard hats and steel-tipped shoes. Smaller dealers will often let you go through the metal jungle with a minimum of cautious words. What can you find? Well, metal sidewalk gratings that you can use for the tops of backyard barbecues; wrought iron fences (especially gates, if you can find them) that make 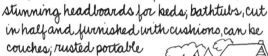 stunning headboards for beds; bathtubs, cut in half and furnished with cushions, can be couches; rusted portable barbecues can do second service as bird feeders; even salvaged fire escapes which someone I know used as a dock at her summer house.

Brass and copper dealers' yards, full of shiny squiggles, are heaven for metal sculptors and macramé artists. Not-so-battered brass musical instruments (trombones, trumpets) make interesting wall sculpture-as is. It's all in how you look at it.

Some scrap yards have stacks of wooden packing boxes. Especially nicely weathered ones make handsome coffee tables. I found some smaller wooden boxes in which books had been shipped ($1 apiece), containing two shelves-perfect bathroom storage cabinets.

Liquidation Companies

Liquidation companies buy outdated equipment from businesses and institutions that are remodeling or going out of business. These are some of my favorite hunting grounds. A sampling of what I have found: Stacks of big round metal hospital trays that double as fast flying saucers in the snow, outdated hospital tray-tables with pop-up mirrors that turn into bedroom dressing tables, copper fire extinguishers I've used as weed holders, metal lockers of all shapes and sizes to hold clothes and toys in kids' rooms (paint them primary colors), wicker and wooden wheelchairs (some people plunk plants in the seats), filing cabinets that are dandy for home offices, glass and wood showcases from stores that can be used to store clothing in your house, post office cubbies destined to be kitchen organizers, wooden restaurant tray tables (now only metal is used) that topped with a tray, make handy plant stands or end tables. One liquidation company I shopped, bought the canvas ballot bags from the city when it switched to using voting machines for elections. The bags were being snapped up by college students to use as dorm laundry bags, duffel bags for kids going off to camp and by managers of Little League teams to haul equipment to the games. Worn plush movie seats could find a home in yours. The egg-crate-like metal covers from fluorescent lighting could be spray painted, stood on end, fastened together, and used as room dividers. The possibilities are endless. Prices in each place depend entirely on the owner and may vary greatly. For the most part, I feel you get your money's worth.

Thrift Stores

Thrift shop shopping for clothing is discussed in the Clothing chapter, but wearables are only a small part of what thrift shops yield. I have always loved their walls of chipped dishes and glassware. For quarters, you can get small pitchers, sugar bowls and vases that are handy to have for flower arranging. Four or five small flowered dishes can be mixed with your own plain set as salad or butter plates. Lamps, too, are good thrift shop finds, especially old brass ones, if you get lucky. Depression furniture—you know, the blond wood, rounded corner kind— dressing tables, wardrobes and bureaus are popularly found at thrift stores. I have seen 30's and 40's white wooden kitchen cabinets with fruit decals and leaking upholstered pieces that could do right fine with a face lift. Odd tables abound. Books and records are easy to come up with.

Again, regularly making the rounds means everything.

Railroad Salvage

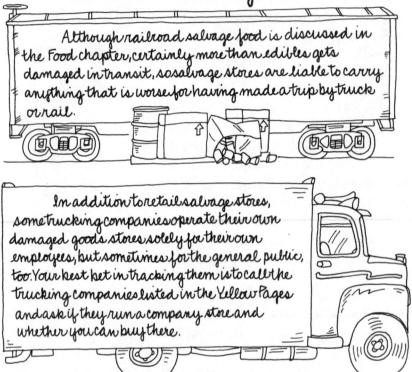

Although railroad salvage food is discussed in the Food chapter, certainly more than edibles gets damaged in transit, so salvage stores are liable to carry anything that is worse for having made a trip by truck or rail.

In addition to retail salvage stores, some trucking companies operate their own damaged goods stores solely for their own employees, but sometimes for the general public, too. Your best bet in tracking them is to call the trucking companies listed in the Yellow Pages and ask if they run a company store and whether you can buy there.

Government Surplus

Government surplus surfaces in both Using the Feds and the Clothing chapters, but to give an added fillip to what you can do with what you find at surplus operations, consider the following.

Ammo pouches leftover from WWI containing a double row

of five pouches can be hung anywhere and planted with ivy. The planters? G.I. glass specimen bottles picked up for a few cents and stuck in each pouch. These same pouches can be used as kitchen spice racks with the specimen bottles holding spices instead of ivy. I have seen Royal Air Force ironstone chamber pots used as handsome soup tureens. Some even have gold trim. Medic corps heating pads, used in the field, need no plugs or batteries to heat up. Just add a couple of spoons of water, shake, and the reusable pad can keep you warm for hours at football games or while you're camping.

An army helmet, hung upside down from a parachute strung from the ceiling can be a planter. A cotton gear hammock, hung in your child's room, can hold his gear. Camouflage material, bought by the yard, turns out nifty bedspreads, shower curtains, wall coverings.

Besides all this, a world of camping equipment, from rucksacks to sleeping bags, can be gleaned from government issue. You can do right well using what the government decides to retire.

Garage Sales and Flea Markets

Garage sales are one of America's fastest-growing phenomena. Besides providing pocket money for enterprising house cleaners, it's a fine place for buyers to pick up bargains. Classified ads in newspapers are good places to find notices of sales, or just keep your eyes open for homemade signs tacked up on poles along the road—mostly on weekends.

At flea markets, sellers rent space at fair grounds, drive-in movies—anywhere one is organized—and sell their wares. Some are small, while others may have hundreds of booths. Scout the newspaper for notices.

Leftovers

Commercial scraps may be just what you're looking for. For instance, Plexiglas fabricators often pile scrap pieces in a corner of the plant and sell them by the square foot or the pound to walk-in customers. You can use small pieces for framing and larger pieces combined with tubing to build tables or shelves.

Frame stores always have odd mat pieces. Ask for them. Leather scraps are often bagged and sold or just thrown in boxes and sold by the piece. Belts? Trim for clothing? Pouches? Wallets?

Lumber companies pile up wood scraps you can take advantage of. Awning makers have odd pieces of new or used canvas. Tote bags? Covers for suitcases on the top of your station wagon on your next car trip?

Used and Abused

Printers are left with ends of the rolls of paper they generally sell for scrap. Most don't want to be bothered by hordes of people asking to buy them, but if you hit someone at the right time, he'll probably sell some rolls to you. Bought by the pound, you'll have years of wrapping paper, shelf paper, and happy kids busy making wall murals.

Any place that produces any product, produces leftovers as well. Seldom advertised for sale, some manufacturers don't even think of them as usable and just scrap them. But true scroungers can put just about any leftover to good use and can obtain just about any leftover-simply by asking for it.

Wholesale

To buy wholesale, you don't need an "inside connection," only ingenuity and assertiveness. You have absolutely nothing to lose by asking a wholesaler if you can buy from him. And the money you save is worth the asking. Just know that if you do business wholesale, you will often have to buy in the same quantities as retailers. This can be a problem if the product is perishable, like fruits and vegetables. Better arrange to share with friends. Also, be direct in your transactions and don't take up a lot of time. If a wholesaler is making up a big retail order and you bother him, you're not going to be welcomed back. I have described here what you may find at some wholesale operations. This list is meant only to whet your appetite.

Fruit and vegetable wholesalers are pretty amenable as long as you buy by the case and don't ask for that one nice head of lettuce you see over there. Cases contain different quantities, according to the size of fruit such as oranges, apples and melons. Many of these businesses also carry Christmas trees, wreaths and

evergreen ropes in December, and
outdoor bedding plants and hanging
baskets in April and May. Bedding
plants must be bought by the flat,
which can contain as many as 96
plants (pansies, petunias, marigolds,
etc.), but hanging baskets (ferns,
begonias, spiders, etc.) can be bought
singly. Before Easter and Mother's

Day, these places are flush with pots of lilies, geraniums, tulips
and chrysanthemums you can also purchase individually. Hours
begin around 3 a.m. when the retail trucks load up, and end in
the early afternoon. It's worth getting up early for.

Canned and frozen food
wholesalers who sell to restaurants
and institutions will sometimes
sell to individuals. Call
around until you
find a friendly
source. A restaurant-size can
may weigh six pounds and serve 20 to 22 people,
while a package of frozen food can weigh 2½
pounds, so be prepared if you have to purchase a case
of these monsters. A good buy is large bags of frozen shrimp for
parties, if the dealer will sell them to you singly. Meanwhile,
some of the people do carry smaller sizes and may break cases
if they're in a good mood.

Restaurant supplies are fabulous. Stock
pots, spoons, spatulas, dishes, baking pans,
glasses—everything for your kitchen.
And because they're made for industrial

use, they are made to last. Look for butcher block tables with stainless steel legs that make perfect dining tables, aluminum pie pans which are great plates to take camping, and glass wine decanters you can use as vases. You can buy many items in single quantities, but you will probably have to buy dishes and glassware by the dozen.

Candyland. Boxes of 48 Hershey bars, Milky Way and Tootsie Rolls - that's only the fattening beginning - from candy wholesalers who will sell to you. Also bubble gum and hard candy pieces in bags of a hundred or more. You can find jars of peanuts and cherries, cartons of gum, cigarettes, and baseball cards, even pantyhose and other items commonly found at candy counters. Superb shopping at Halloween.

Industrial cleaning compounds are more potent and durable than products made for home use. Think of what a formula devised to clean a supermarket floor will do in your kitchen! Janitorial suppliers will also sell you mops, brooms, brushes, detergents,

Wholesale

rug and upholstery shampoos, insecticides, cement and asphalt sealer as well as every cleaning compound imaginable.

Paper wholesalers yield paper towels, toilet paper, plates, cups and other picnic accessories. At industrial rubber suppliers, you can find heavy-duty raincoats, slickers, gloves, mats, zillions of boots, foam rubber slabs and all kinds of hoses and fittings you may need around the house.

Basket suppliers who sell to fruit stores and florists may also sell to you. Great picnic hampers here. This is also the place to start when you put together your own fruit baskets at Christmas. (Next stop, fruit and vegetable wholesalers.) Party favors including balloons, masks, horns, you-name-it, are available at novelty companies. Rope and string purchased from industrial rope suppliers will save you plenty if you macramé. Having a brunch? Check a smoked fish wholesaler to see if you can buy salmon, lox and whitefish. (Five pounds is usually the minimum.) Chances are he'll carry some other kinds of food, like cheese in big blocks, too. Investigate popcorn wholesalers. Yes, the ones that sell to movie chains and amusement parks will also sell to you.

The wholesale scene is as endless as the sources you uncover in the Yellow Pages. Look up the product you want to buy and the wholesalers will be plainly listed. Get up your nerve, get on the phone and ask if you can buy it - wholesale.

Factory Outlets

Chasing "famous label" merchandise at the Mill Outlet Store or the Ladies' Factory Outlet or the Famous Brand Outlet or whatever name a factory outlet calls itself can be rewarding or just plain frustrating. If the "famous label" merchandise turns out to be the brand of dress or suit you normally buy retail or always wanted to buy retail but couldn't afford, and is now available at less than retail price you've found a real bargain. On the other hand, if it's cheap stuff you wouldn't want at any price, you've wasted your time.

That's all part of playing factory outlet hopscotch. When you go to the Mill Outlet Store, you will often find it is on the premises of a nationally known manufacturing company. The reason the name is withheld is because the manufacturer's main customers are retail stores, who aren't going to be thrilled to learn a manufacturer who sells to them is openly advertising and offering the same dresses for half the price. In addition to selling quietly, manufacturers also soothe the angry retailers by claiming they are "selling only flawed merchandise or last year's

Factory Outlets

goods". They would "certainly not dream of selling first-run quality to compete with the retailers." Judge for yourself. Factory outlet merchandise can be slightly flawed, perfect, or a real disaster. It can definitely be goods from several seasons ago or today's fashions. But what is a factory outlet anyway?

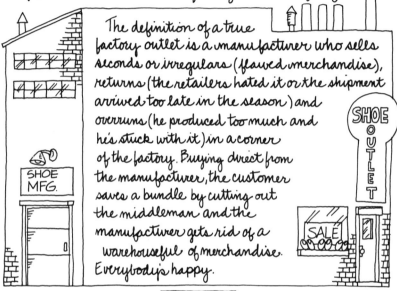

The definition of a true factory outlet is a manufacturer who sells seconds or irregulars (flawed merchandise), returns (the retailers hated it or the shipment arrived too late in the season) and overruns (he produced too much and he's stuck with it) in a corner of the factory. Buying direct from the manufacturer, the customer saves a bundle by cutting out the middleman and the manufacturer gets rid of a warehouseful of merchandise. Everybody's happy.

Some manufacturers, however, do not operate their own factory outlet stores. But they still have to get rid of their seconds and leftovers, so they sell them to other store operators, who may buy seconds and overproduced merchandise from a number of manufacturers. Some of these people may call their stores factory outlets. Others may call their operations manufacturers' outlets, factory stores or even manufacturers' courtesy stores. In the truest sense, they are retailers. Sure, they are buying goods at low prices and selling them cheaper than you can buy at a regular retail store, but they are not factory outlets. Can you save money at them? Of course. Just be sure you know the retail value of what you are shopping for so you can determine how much of a good deal you are getting.

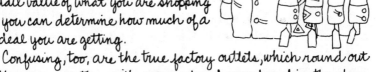

Confusing, too, are the true factory outlets, which round out what they manufacture with overproduced merchandise they buy from other suppliers. For instance, a shirt company may buy trousers from another manufacturer to allow factory outlet customers to buy complete outfits. This one-stop shopping increases his sales. Is this place still a true factory outlet? Yes and no. He's selling _his_ merchandise direct, but retailing another's—even though at cut-rate prices. It's very sticky.

Some manufacturers may also operate strings of factory outlets across the country in strategically placed high-traffic shopping areas. Carter's infants clothing and the Bass and Dexter shoe companies are good examples.

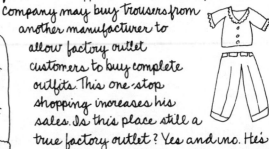

They are factory outlets relative to their own brands even though they aren't located at the factory. Like the shirt company mentioned above, some round out

56

Factory Outlets

their merchandise with other manufacturers' goods. Confusing. But as the whole factory outlet scene has grown in popularity, it has changed to meet the needs of people who are retreating from traditional stores and higher prices to no-frills direct-to-the-customer operations where you get a crack at lower prices.

If you find a factory outlet where you are able to buy quality merchandise at a savings, this will offset some of the inconveniences of shopping at these places. (I will endure lots of inconveniences for great-looking cashmere sweaters, suits made by one of the manufacturers who supplies Brooks Brothers, and comforters that didn't quite make it to Bloomingdale's.) Many are cash-and-carry operations, have no dressing rooms or at best have a communal one. Labels are often cut out of clothing and everything is buy as is. But as factory outlets are coming out of the closet, more amenities are being offered. At some, you can now use credit cards and even return merchandise.

In some cities, factory outlets cluster in one area. Reading, Pennsylvania boasts streets of factory outlets. Trains

and chartered buses bring shoppers there from hundreds of miles away. Hollandale, Miami Beach and Lauderdale Lakes, Florida offer huge shopping centers filled with stores selling bargain-priced manufacturers' close-outs and clearance merchandise. A whole new era has been reached with the advent of Consumer Outlet Marts. One in Youngstown, Ohio has merchandise from 57 factories under a single roof. More of these operations are popping up in cities all over the United States.

The factory outlet trend may be mushrooming, but discounting has been going on for as long as people have run competitive businesses. For instance, Orchard Street on New York's Lower East Side has been bargain paradise forever. You can go through racks at Saks', Bergdorf's and any other prestige store and then shop the hundreds of stores on Orchard Street and see the same label merchandise—this year's merchandise—for a fraction of the cost. How do they do it? The Orchard Street stores don't have Bergdorf's rent to pay, nor do they offer the niceties or the services, so they can afford to mark down the prices. The whole scene is fabulous.

58

Factory Outlets

Discounters are in every city in the country.

Sometimes you can take advantage of especially good deals made by department stores or other retail operations. Any smart merchandiser is always on the lookout for special purchases. One way he gets them is to wait until a season is just about to begin and then buy merchandise at low prices the manufacturer is stuck with. Buying a season ahead is more costly. Close-outs and seconds also find their way into department store sales or in their warehouse stores along with scratched and dented merchandise, floor samples and other leftover stock. Warehouse stores have always been great places to shop.

Sears and Roebuck, Montgomery Ward and other large mail order houses run surplus liquidation centers across the country where returned, damaged and leftover merchandise is sold at cheaper than retail prices. To find out if one is in your city, look up "Mail Order Houses"

in the Yellow Pages and ask the manager if there is also a
liquidation center nearby. Another Yellow Page listing where
liquidation centers may lurk is "Retail Distribution
Centers". Check both.

Sample shops are burgeoning. A salesman
shows samples to retailers seasons ahead
of when they will appear in the store.
Then he sells his samples to make room
for the next season's round of calls. Shops
buy salesmen's merchandise and wind
up with a supply of clothes more
current then the regular retail stores,
which they often discount more than 25 percent.

These are some of the most common outlet types where
you can stretch your shopping dollar. The main thing to
remember at all of them is to examine
whatever you buy very carefully. If a second
is too far gone, it won't be repairable and,
if you didn't notice the extent of the
damage, you're going to be stuck with
something you can't use. Another thing.
Just because something is below retail price, people will often buy
it whether they need it or not, whether they even like it or not. I
bought a dress that was too big and I knew it. But I bought it
anyway because it was so cheap. I hated wearing that dress
because I could never get it to fit right and I wound up giving it
away. Not exactly a classic example of a good buy.

How to find factory outlets, discount
stores, sample shops, retailers selling
at below regular retail prices? Here are

Factory Outlets

some ways to begin. First check your newspaper for Mill Outlet, Factory Outlet or Salesman's Sample Sale ads. Then check the Yellow Pages under the product you are looking for. There is usually no factory outlet listing in the phone book. However, if you look under "Men's Furnishings" or "Ladies' Apparel," you may strike gold and find mill outlets and sample shops listed. If you go to one of these places, you will sometimes find lists of area factory outlets on the counter. Ask the sales clerks for names of other outlets. Ask other shoppers. People who shop outlets know where the good places are.

Sometimes your chamber of commerce or convention bureau has lists of factory outlets and discount shops. They may be promoting them to visitors to your city. It doesn't hurt to ask.

Local guides listing "inside shopping places" are on the upswing. Seattle's Super Shopper describes more than 350 places to buy practically everything for less in all kinds of appealing places, from egg farms and canneries to discount clothing stores. There are popular guides in Detroit, Chicago, Indianapolis, New York and Cincinnati - to name only a smattering. Ask at your local bookstore if your city has a shopping guide.

There are also some national guides that will help you finger factory outlets. Jean Bird has written six separate Factory Outlet Shopping Guides for New York/Long Island/Westchester,

New England States, Eastern Pennsylvania, New Jersey/Rockland County, Washington D.C. Region, The Carolinas. (Each is $2.95) She gives descriptions of stores, hours, phone numbers, directions on how to get to each and the percent you save. These books are available in bookstores and libraries or write to F.O.S.G. Publications Publishers, Box 95V, Oradell, New Jersey 07649.

Annie Moldafsky's <u>Good Buy Book</u> covers bargain hunting in Illinois, Michigan, Indiana, Wisconsin and Ohio. She mentions some brand names found at outlets besides listing what conveniences, such as fitting rooms, you will find. This paperback ($2.95) is at bookstores and libraries, or write to Swallow Press, 811 West Junior Terrace, Chicago, Illinois 60613.

The <u>S.O.S. Directory</u>, compiled by Iris Ellis, $5.95, is a directory of shopper-recommended outlet stores from coast to coast. Listings are brief, some mention brands sold, and an updated version appears on the market each year.

S.O.S. also maintains a shopping service. If you call or write to them before you plan a trip, they will tell you of major outlets in the area you plan to visit or on your route along the way. They also arrange factory outlet shopping excursions in the Florida area. S.O.S. is available at bookstores, libraries, or by writing to <u>S.O.S. Directory</u>, P.O. Box 10482, Jacksonville, Florida 32207. Phone (not collect) 1-904-399-5956.

Guerrilla Shopping Tactics

Today's consumers have more allies than ever to aid them if they are unfairly dealt with in a business transaction. City consumer agencies, state attorney generals, small claims courts, even federal agencies all offer recourse. And it is comforting to know they exist, because at some time or other, we may have to turn to one of them. However, there are some simple things that we can do to protect ourselves from getting ripped off in the first place. Begin by being informed.

If you are buying a major appliance which will require a major investment, do some research before you reach in your pocket and commit yourself. There are reputable consumer magazines in every library which list the merits and failures of most products on the market. That way, you'll know-in advance of your purchase- what you will be getting.

There are shelves of consumer books in the library and in bookstores containing information on subjects ranging from which cosmetics contain which ingredients to how to select storm doors and windows. What is not covered in these books and magazines may be found in the thousands of government consumer brochures. Information is available everywhere. Use it. Then go shopping. But even while you're in the stores, ask questions for your own protection.

Before you make a purchase, ask what the return policy of the store is. If it's an "all sales are final" place, you may want to reconsider being a customer. Some stores may give you a credit in the store rather than cash for returned goods while others unhesitatingly give refunds, credits, make exchanges and return deposits. Trade in those stores that give you the privileges you want.

ALL SALES FINAL!

Ask if the store guarantees what you are buying. For how long? Is there a factory warranty? Are there labor, installation or delivery charges? Just who is responsible for fixing what you buy if it conks out? And don't accept verbal guarantees. Get them in writing.

If you are signing a contract, really read it first. If there's something you don't understand written in it, make sure you do before you commit yourself. Don't be embarrassed about asking. Better to be embarrassed than sorry later.

Save sales slips and cash register slips if you make a cash purchase so you have a record of what you buy. If you're a charge customer and lose your sales slip, the store can duplicate it. If you pay cash and have no record of a purchase you want to return, you may be out of luck.

Guerrilla Shopping Tactics

If you wish to return a purchase, and you are entitled to do so, go first to the department where you bought it. If you get grief from a sales clerk, ask for the buyer of the department. Still no satisfaction? Head for Customer Service. 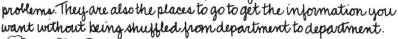 Many people do not realize there is such a department in most large department stores. I didn't, but I was sure glad when I discovered it. The chief function of these departments is simply to keep customers happy. (Hurray!) So they act as a buffer between the merchandisers and the customers, solving problems. They are also the places to go to get the information you want without being shuffled from department to department.

As an example of how Customer Service can help, let me cite the saga of my flame-throwing iron. It did this routine a month after I bought it at a large department store, so I took it back. I was directed to the repair department and was informed I would either have a repaired iron or a new one within two weeks. After two weeks had passed, and I had neither, I phoned the store's repair department. I was told to call the manufacturer's repair department where my iron was currently hospitalized. I did. They said they never received my iron. I called the store once more and was told they would trace my iron. My temperature started to rise. I needed an iron to use and I was getting tired of the runaround. In an effort to be accommodating, the repair clerk offered me a loaner iron, but said I would have to come downtown to pick it up, and of course, return it, when I finally received mine. I was tied up and didn't have the time to go downtown and the repair clerk would not send one to me. I called Customer Service. The next day, I received a new iron delivered to my door. Happy ending? Not quite. The new iron heated to only one temperature—fry. This time, my husband took the iron downtown and after recounting the story, again, the repair clerk called the buyer of the small appliance department who presented my husband with a new iron. The third one. So far, it works.

Although there is a lot of aggravation involved in this story, it does show that Customer Service is a good red-tape cutter. Also, it shows that reputable stores stand behind their merchandise and try to keep customers satisfied. Maybe you pay more at them than at "Discount Heaven" but because products go on the fritz so quickly and so often these days, you are ahead in the long run, if you buy from people who will stand behind what they sell.

If it's improper billing that is driving you crazy, don't do battle with a computer. If you wrote once describing the error only to receive the same wrong bill again, call Customer Service or the credit department and talk to a human being. Don't cut up your charge card or mutilate computer cards and mail them back to the store in a frenzy. Call someone responsible, have the bill, your account number and other pertinent information handy, and get the mistake settled.

Guerrilla Shopping Tactics

Always ask for the name of the person you are speaking to on the phone. Identify yourself, too. This puts the conversation on a more personal level and gives you someone specific to refer to if you don't get the answers from him. If you get put off, ask to speak to the person's immediate superior. And then his. Go to the top, if you have to. Be polite, but positive and firm. Don't yell, but don't take no for an answer.

On the other hand, if you are pleased with a sales person or any individual you have dealt with in a large company, write a letter to his boss telling him of your pleasure. That person will be yours forever. Talk about service! If you can establish  a relationship with a salesperson, that person will call you when special things come in; tell you when the pair of shoes you have been lusting after all winter is about to go on sale, even save things for you.

Sometimes it pays to comparison shop the cost of something you want at several stores. If a blouse is on sale at one store, but you would rather buy it at the department store you regularly patronize, your store may meet their competitor's price if you tell them about it. Also know that if you buy an item at regular price and it goes on sale within three weeks of your purchase, many stores will honor the sale price and credit you with the difference. Nice.

Buying a service? That's where many headaches begin. Most of us are helpless victims of T.V. repairmen or car mechanics because we don't "speak the language." It's easy to be taken advantage of when you don't know a spark plug from a generator. Consumer advocates, who say that service-related complaints are among the most numerous they receive, advise that you ask friends who they use to fix their car, their TV, their furnace. Are they happy with the service? Satisfied customers are the best reference. But also ask the person who is about to seal your driveway or remodel your basement for his references. Make sure they are not setups by asking to see the jobs he's done. If he won't give you names, write him off. Another way to find reputable service people is to call the distributor of the product you have bought in your city and ask for the names of the authorized service companies. What good is repair work guaranteed for six months if the repair work is rotten to begin with? Again, the guarantee is only as good as the guy who stands behind it. Don't pick services blindly.

Courts of Last Resort

If you've tried being reasonable with the people you have dealt with, from the sales clerk to the president of the store, from the serviceman to the owner of the company, and you still are dissatisfied, start pulling out all the stops.

Guerrilla Shopping Tactics

Compose letters which state all the pertinent information concerning the transaction: the date, the name and model number of the product or the situation or the service, the name of the person or the company you dealt with, how much you paid, whether you bought or signed a contract and the nature of your complaint. If you can, enclose copies (never the original) of any advertisement, labels or additional material that will substantiate your claim. Send copies of these letters to the consumer protection agency in your city, if it has one. If not, write to the Consumer Protection Division in the Office of the Attorney General of your state. Another resource is the director of the Office of Consumer Affairs, Executive Office of the President, Washington, D.C. 20506. Call or write your local Better Business Bureau. They confront the company with your complaint. (Better yet, call the BBB for information about a company's status before you do business with it.)

Does your local newspaper have an Action Line or Consumer Alert column? Some TV stations employ consumer investigating troubleshooters as part of their news programs. Contact these people.

ON THE AIR

BUSINESS OFFICE

Get to the places where the company you are quarreling with may advertise. Write to newspapers, radio and television stations and tell them how you have been unfairly treated by one of their advertisers. Send carbon copies of all your complaint letters to the company you are fighting so they can see the pressure you are exerting. Most hate adverse publicity and may settle just to shut you up.

Don't stop yet. Write to your State Representatives, State Senators, U.S. Representatives and Senators. Call the Federal Information Center in your city to find out what other federal agencies may be able to help you.

Think all this is a bother and takes an inordinate amount of time? You're right. That's why a lot of people shake their heads, take a beating and walk away from the situation. Only you can decide if going through all of this is worth it.

Hiring an attorney as a final resort is costly. Maybe more costly than the sum you hope to recover. Small claims courts, though, may provide a solution since they are set up to resolve disputes involving claims of $300 to $3,000 (this varies from state to state.) Filing does not require an attorney, and generally, the fee for the process should not run over $5.

To obtain information on the procedure you must follow, call the Clerks of Courts in your city or county. If there is a consumer protection agency, they may also have printed matter and advice on filing small claims.

Guerrilla Shopping Tactics

The main thing to remember is to prepare a strong case for court by bringing receipts, bills, cancelled checks, estimates, contracts, even witnesses with you. If you win your claim, your opponent is legally obligated to pay you the amount of the judgment and if he pays you voluntarily, your troubles are over. If not, you will have to take additional legal steps to collect the money owed you. Again, obtain this information from the Clerk of Courts.

Is it worth it? You'll probably lose a day's pay waiting for your case to be called, and even if you win, you have to go through more legal hassles to get your money. It's tough.

One head of a metropolitan consumer protection division told me he cautions consumers to be careful before they buy, to be wary, informed and intelligent to avoid all the hassles. His parting words, "Remember, anything or any deal that sounds too good to be true, probably is." Too bad.

71

Food

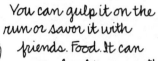

You can gulp it on the run or savor it with friends. Food. It can ease loneliness, soothe frustrations, be a treat, a reward, a sharing social experience. What many of us forget is that its main purpose is to provide nourishment to keep our bodies healthy. How to nourish our bodies best is the subject of continuing controversy.

There are as many opinions on what you should and should not eat as there are experts in the field of nutrition and medicine. Few of them ever agree. Where does that leave you—bombarded by the newspaper's latest bad food news on the atrocities of food additives and staggered by the do-not-eat-it list, which grows longer daily. Hope sprouts anew in special diet books written by experts which promise The Answers until they are, in turn, displaced by the latest "expert" who has an even Better Answer. Junk food and health food proponents square off while natural food stores take on finger-lickin'-good chicken and have-it-your-way hamburgers. Facing danger every time we put something that tastes good in our mouths, whom do we believe?

In an effort to find some simple, easy-to-live-with answers, I consulted with nutritionists, dietitians, home economists and doctors. Most of them agreed that the key to a proper diet is to eat a variety of foods, in moderation. The greater the number of foods on your menu, particularly those that are not heavily processed, the less chance there is that you will be deficient in the nutrients you need.

An unequivocal approach to food is unrealistic. People get scared and do drastic things. For instance, because eggs contain high levels of cholesterol, people stop eating them altogether. But, at the same time they swear off eggs, they continue eating ice cream and cake and fatty meats which overflow with cholesterol. It just doesn't make sense.

Step back, look at your lifestyle, think about how much exercise you get daily, consider what diseases are hereditary in your family, how much you weigh, what things you like to eat, and make intelligent decisions based on facts. See a doctor and get a checkup. Find out what your cholesterol level is before you never eat another egg. And don't go to the bookstore and grab the latest fad diet book as the best solution.

Easy Alternatives

As you examine your daily eating habits and find that some are not as healthy as they should be, look for still-pleasing alternatives. If you are addicted to a 10 a.m. coffee and doughnut,

Living Better

try to substitute juice and maybe a bran muffin instead. Juice will give you nourishment coffee doesn't, and the bran muffin provides fiber and trace minerals instead of the ever present fat in doughnuts.

If you love yogurt, you can make it even better by buying the plain variety and mixing it with fresh fruit, instead of buying the flavored kind which dumps a lot of sugar into your system. Bananas and citrus fruits are always available as mixes even in the winter. In summer, you can take your pick of the crop.

We are becoming a nation of fatties because our diets are packed with fat-producing foods. At the same time, we hold increasingly sedentary jobs and don't get a chance to burn up the fat we ingest. So, we have to moderate our diets. Substitute. Sensibly. And get off our fannies and walk four blocks to the store instead of driving. Or use the steps instead of the elevator.

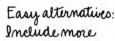

Easy alternatives: Include more poultry and fish in your meals instead of red meat. If you do buy red meat, choose lean cuts. That's an easy way to reduce fat consumption. Get carbohydrates from fresh fruits and vegetables instead of sugar. Try to include more whole grains and cereals in your diet and take a look at the amount of dairy products you use. I'm not suggesting eliminating them—that's for you to decide, based on your health and your diet. If substitutes aren't palatable to you (they aren't to me), simply use less. Sugar lurks in many prepared foods and we sure don't need as much as we are getting. Start reading labels. A can of pineapple rings packed in extra-heavy syrup means it is loaded with sugar. Look for the kind packed in its natural juice.

We are creatures of habit—many of them bad. We're in a hurry. No time for lunch, so we grab a hamburger from a nearby fast-food emporium. Contrary to the opinion of some people, you will not die from a lunch consisting of a quickie hamburger, french fries and a chocolate shake.

But, at the same time, know that you have just polished off a calorie-packed lunch, high in fat in proportion to the other nutrients it contains. Even if you can afford these calories, eat a piece of fruit for dessert to round out the menu and to provide the missing nutrients. And remember variety. If you find yourself eating on the run more frequently, think about occasionally packing your lunch instead. A lunch that contains different ingredients from the fast-food hamburger. Then take a walk around the block.

Too much of any one thing, even if it's considered healthy for you, can have ill effects. I love the story one of the dietitians I talked to told on herself. She was so concerned that her newborn baby got the Vitamin A she wanted her to have, she poured on the carrots—that is, until the baby began taking on a decidedly yellow glow. Gulp.

Palatable Diet Books

What about all those books hatched by the hundreds dealing with every kind of special diet imaginable? How can you

intelligently decide if any is valid? Use these guidelines.

Look at the author's background. Is his training in nutrition from a recognized university? If the author has the title of doctor, does it mean he is an M.D. or a Ph.D. in ancient history? Is the work endorsed by the American Dietetic Association or the American Medical Association? If the author is not a nutritionist, does he acknowledge the advice of recognized nutritionists? Who are the author's sources of information? Does he have a bibliography? Or is he the only voice of authority? Are the claims of the author reasonable and justifiable? (No, you cannot lose 48 pounds by eating grapefruit for 48 hours, as nice as that would be to believe.) Does the book use vague medical terms and give fuzzy, unsupported promises?

Food

Is the author trying to sell you a product? One that just happens to be his? If you ask all these questions of a book, you'll be able to make a more intelligent buying decision.

Label Reading

Another smart thing you can do is to start reading-really reading-the labels on what you buy in the supermarket, and understand what they mean. Ingredients are listed on the package in the order of their profusion. If you buy a can of beef stew which lists gravy first, then potatoes, carrots, peas and meat, you'll know that you're getting the most of what you least think is inside. If your box of cereal lists sugar as the first ingredient, put it back on the shelf. If the sugar content on any can or package is broken down into white sugar, brown sugar, dextrose, corn syrup and corn sugar so that the ingredients appear further down on the list of contents because of their smaller quantities, add them up yourself and come up with your own answers. This is a manufacturer's favorite way to disguise sugar content.

Know that if you buy apple juice, the bottle should contain 100% pure juice. If it says apple juice drink, you are getting only 50% juice. If it says appleade,

77

apple punch or apple flavored drink, you're getting mostly water, sugar and additives. Go for the real thing.

Use labels to select foods that give you the nutrients you need daily. The amount of each nutrient is listed on the package along with the caloric content. You can also use labels to make sure you're getting the most for your food dollar. Two frozen pot pies of the same weight may vary in price by a few cents. Read the nutrition label to see which has the higher percentage of protein. For a few cents more, you may be getting a better meal.

Then there's the whole question of food additives. While we depend on what's in cans and cardboard packages to provide a good portion of what we eat, reading the alphabet soup of additives listed on the labels is pretty depressing. And confusing, since most of us haven't the foggiest idea of what they really mean and what they can do to us. It's easy to get scared. Instead, be informed. A good way to do that is to use <u>Eater's Digest, The Consumer's Factbook of Food Additives</u> by Michael Jacobsen, #1.95, Doubleday Anchor paperback, to look up what you want to know. The book is written in clear language and singles out the most widespread, the most useful and the most questionable additives.

Many of us don't have time to shop at ten different specialty stores for so-called "natural foods," which are often

Food

very expensive. And sometimes not as natural as they claim. But what we can do, is to make the most of what is on the supermarket shelves by being better informed. These two paperbacks (which do not always agree on some facts) can help you be a better supermarket shopper. They are The Complete Food Handbook by Roger P. Doyle and James L. Redding, $2.45, Grove Press, and The Supermarket Handbook, Nikki and David Goldbeck, $1.95, Signet.

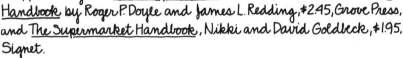

Junk Food

Fritos and Hershey Bars and Milky Ways and all those good things we love to snack on. Why are they classified as junk food? Because, according to Michael Lasky, author of The Complete Junk Food Book, $7.95, McGraw-Hill, any food that relies on sugar and/or fat as its primary ingredient, supplying very few nutrients in comparison to the calories it provides, is junk food. Empty calories. We eat a lot, but wind up undernourished and fat. Instead of heading for the candy machine when you get hungry in the middle of the afternoon, reach in your desk drawer and pull out an apple. Not as exciting, for sure. But who says you have to do it every day?

An occasional treat can't hurt unless you are on a strict diet. (Who can live in a world without M&M's?) The main thing to remember is to not let junk food be the only food you eat. It can be an occasional and delightful addition.

For a good look at junk food, read Michael Lasky's book. He rates everything from fast food restaurants, candy and ice cream to puddings, crackers and chips. All their contents are listed. He even institutes a Junk Food Hall of Fame in which he enshrines the best of the tooth rotters. Informative and fun reading.

Shopping

Everyone has his own favorite shopping methods. Some of us are weekly planners, while others are five o'clock shoppers. Whatever. Because food prices are so high, no matter which method we use, we all have to be smart consumers. Read the food ads in the paper. If the weekly special happens to be one of your favorites, you're in luck. But don't overstock either. You may get sick of eating your "special" after awhile and your bargain may backfire. Also, don't buy a bargain just because it is. You'll end up with a pantryful of food nobody likes. Again, be a label reader. Make sure the expiration date gives you enough time to eat the food before it spoils. And try not to shop when you're hungry. You often wind up with a basketful of snacks instead of nutritious ingredients for meals.

Buying food in season is another budget saver. The price of

Food

strawberries in winter is a killer, but the cost of corn, in season, is
a delight. Think about
freezing fruit and vegetables
when they are plentiful and
cheaper so you can have them
in winter. Put blueberries
on a baking sheet in the
freezer so they freeze individually
instead of in clumps. Then put them

in a plastic bag. True, the defrosted consistency is not the same as
when they are fresh, but they sure look good to me on cereal in winter
when I just can't look another banana in the eye.

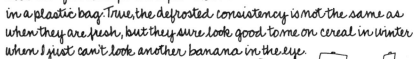

Shopping at fruit and vegetable wholesalers and sharing
with friends is another way to beat high food prices. More about
that is found in the Wholesale chapter.

Shopping railroad salvage
food stores is another money-
saver. Food cartons damaged
in transit by trains and
trucks are bought by store
owners and offered for sale.
You can get good deals at many
of these places, but know how to
examine a damaged can to see if
it is safe for you to use. If the seams
are ruptured or the can leaks
or is expanded, don't buy it. The
food inside has been exposed to
outside bacteria, and you are

taking a chance on food poisoning. If the can is rusted on the outside, look out, it may be rusted all the way through, spoiling the food.

Labels are often missing at some of these places, so you may be buying mystery food. If you're queasy about any of it, look for good buys on cleansers, paper products and other inedibles. Those can't hurt anyone.

Food co-ops are also popular alternatives. Many start as a group of people who share produce and then grow into complete food stores. Often co-ops stock whole grains and flour not

commonly found in supermarkets because members are concerned with good nutrition. Two excellent sources of co-op information that even list existing co-ops by state are *The Food Co-op Handbook: How to Bypass Supermarkets and Control the Quality and Price of Your Food* by the Co-op Handbook Collective, Houghton-Mifflin, and *How to Start Your Own Food Co-op, A Guide to Wholesale Buying,* Gloria Stern, Walker and Co., each a $4.95 paperback.

Found Food

There are lots of throwaways in the kitchen that you can retrieve to make meals thriftier and more nutritious. What to do with four beans, a handful of peas and a few cooked carrots? Lots of things. Accumulate them in a bag in the freezer and stop buying frozen mixed vegetables. You've got your own to enrich

Food

canned vegetable soup or to use in casseroles along with leftover meat. Put a can of consommé or tomato soup in the blender with leftover cooked vegetables. Blend a few seconds, add water or milk, heat and serve. You've got a cup of handy nutritious soup for lunch.

Save leftover juices when you boil vegetables, too. Use them when you make soup instead of water. Get the benefit of all those vitamins. Also, when cooking vegetables, try to cut down the cooking time. The more you cook, the less nutritious your food becomes. Frozen food, already blanched, never needs as much cooking time as it says on the package. And don't use as much water as they call for either. Stop throwing away the liquid from canned vegetables, too. This liquid is a good candidate for your soup pot, or add it to tomato juice in the blender for a veggie cocktail.

Save fruit odds and ends in the freezer, too. Use them to mix with yogurt, sprinkle over ice cream or blend with milk for shakes. Pour leftover coffee in ice cube trays and freeze. Flavor milk with a coffee ice cube or use them in iced coffee if you like yours strong (instead of regular ice, which dilutes it).

When you unwrap a stick of butter you can use the wrapper to grease your baking pan. You usually use only dabs of

83

Living Better

tomato paste at a time and wind up wasting a whole can when you open it. Keep tomato paste in a plastic container in the freezer and carve out a piece whenever you need it.

Apple peels can be used to make jelly. Cookie crumbs and broken cookies left in the bottom of the bag can be sprinkled over ice cream. Leftover pancake batter? Make extra pancakes, wrap them individually and freeze. Pop them frozen in the toaster and you can enjoy "Sunday breakfasts" any day of the week. Jam or jelly jar empty except for all the good stuff sticking to the sides? Fill the jar with milk, shake, and you've got an instant strawberry, blueberry, or whatever milkshake.

Grate the rind from lemons and oranges before squeezing them and freeze it. You will have citrus rind ready whenever your recipe calls for it.

Brown bag tips. Keep your bread frozen and make your sandwiches on frozen slices which will defrost and be fresh tasting in time for lunch. Frozen bread slices will also keep the lunchmeat cooler and help prevent quick spoilage if you can't refrigerate your lunch. Also, if you use mustard, spread it between the meat slices rather than on the bread so it won't get soggy.

Make your own bread crumbs in the blender from odds

Food

and ends of loaves you store in the freezer. Store-bought bread crumbs have the consistency of sand. Bread leftovers can turn up as croutons to top salads and soups, too.

Prepared salad dressings are craziness. Buy your own oil and vinegar, add a few spices and you've got it. This brings up the whole subject of convenience foods. How inconvenient is it, really, to open two bottles (oil and vinegar) instead of one? You're paying so much more for something that is done for you when it's just as simple to do it yourself. The more completely prepared the food is, the more expensive it's likely to be. You are paying for someone else to do the cooking for you when what you could do yourself is cheaper and probably a lot tastier.

SUPER MEAL
JUST HEAT!!

Many of us are busy and don't have time to prepare intricate meals at the end of a working day. And working is as important to me as it is to many others these days, but so is eating well. Coming home to a hamburger in a bag or popping a tasteless frozen dinner in the oven just isn't worth coming home to. You can make healthy, tasty meals in minutes. The trick is being organized.

Living Better

Once a week, before I go grocery shopping, my husband, my children and I decide what we'd like to eat that week. Simple things that demand little preparation time which everyone shares in our family. Fresh vegetables that take only minutes to cook. Fish and meat and chicken to broil. Salads. Even cans of soup I doctor up to taste better coupled with a green salad and cheese toast. As long as the meal consists of hearty food that looks pretty on the table, kind conversation and sharing, isn't that really what its all about?

Reliable Sources of Nutrition Information

These books have been favorably reviewed by noted nutritionists in the publications of the American Dietetic Association and the Society for Nutrition Education.

A Diet for Living, Jean Mayer, David McKay
Realities of Nutrition, Ronald Deutsch, Bull Publishing Co.
Food, Nutrition and You, F. Clydesdale and F. Francis, Prentice-Hall

Food

The New Nuts Among the Berries, Ronald Deutsch, Bull
Publishing Co.
Nutrition for the Growing Years, Margaret McWilliams, John
Wiley and Sons
Processed Foods and the Consumer: Additives, Labeling, Standards,
and Nutrition, Vernal S. Packard, University of
Minnesota Press
Panic in the Pantry, Elizabeth Whelan and Frederick Stare, Atheneum
Keeping Food Safe, Hassell Bradley and Carole Sundberg,
Doubleday & Co.
Diet for a Small Planet, Frances Moore Lappé, Ballantine
Recipes for a Small Planet, Ellen Ewald, Ballantine

National organizations that can be contacted for reliable
pamphlets on nutrition:

American Dietetic Association
430 N. Michigan Avenue
Chicago, Illinois 60611

Consumer Information
Public Documents Distribution Center
Pueblo, Colorado 81009

Public Affairs Pamphlets
381 Park Avenue South
New York, New York 10016

American Medical Association and American
Dental Association addresses are listed in Keys to the City.

Nutrition and food preparation information is available from
your Department of Agriculture county agent. Look in the Using the
Feds chapter of this book for more of what he offers and for information
on how to find your county agent.

87

Clothing

Clothes. I have loved them from the moment I wore my first velvet dress with the lace Peter Pan collar. I will always love the feel of good fabric, the cut of a great looking jacket, trying on a dress and knowing it's exactly right for The Occasion, having it fit perfectly, feeling smart in it, buying something beautiful I love and also sensing I've made a good investment. Unfortunately, this happens less and less these days.

I find a blouse I like only to discover the price is about what I paid for a jacket a couple of seasons ago. (Yes, I know, even Volkswagens are higher.) I go crazy when a couple of the buttons give up and fall off when I fasten them. I put the blouse back on the rack and search for another only to find that all of them are in some state of disrepair. Sad. No, maddening. As prices skyrocket, quality seems to drop just as quickly. We all need to clothe ourselves one way or another, so what do we do? Here are some answers.

According to designers, clothing merchandisers, fashion directors and tailors, American women buy "a look." A high-styled fashionable look created by designers, reflected in fashion

"BUYMORE LTD."—OUR NEW LOOK IS HERE!

magazines and department stores, and changeable with the seasons. Expensive as it is for women who want to capture "the look", it's also expensive for the manufacturers who have to gear up and produce different styles each season.

Men's suits—good traditional ones—can last for years. Their style hardly changes. Men's clothing manufacturers don't have to invest in the expense of retooling each season and can spend money instead on handsome fabric and better quality workmanship. The cut of a ladies' jacket may be slim this year, bulky the next. And if women don't especially like the "new look", the stores are going to get stuck with it. Certainly, if the stores aren't buying, the manufacturers will take a beating, too. So style is dangerous. And the price of this danger is built into the garment. Because fashion turnover on ladies' ready-to-wear is so fast, and demands can change so quickly, the time is not spent on how well the garment is put together since this will pad even further an already sky-high price. It is invested in creating that ever-changing, sought after "look." The verdict? The less-quality ladies' jacket often costs more than the well-put-together men's.

Living Better

Women are also label happy. (Men, more and more, too.) Not only do they like to buy prestige designers' creations, they seem to like it even better if the designer's name is plastered all over the garment itself. And for the privilege of wearing the designer's name, they are willing to pay just about anything. Heaven help us!

A professor of fashion merchandising I spoke to told me she instructs her students to merchandise their own closets as they would a clothing department in a store. Each season, take inventory of what you own and know exactly what you need to buy to fill in the fashion gaps in your closet. Instead of buying a whole new look each season (who can afford it?), update last year's skirt with this year's jacket or blouse or scarf.

Fall into a color range. Browns, beiges and taupes need fewer pairs of shoes and purses than if your clothes run the rainbow gamut. Look for separates. Classic shirts, blazers, sweaters and skirts have longer lives than trendy dresses. Examine your lifestyle carefully. If you go to an office every day and come home happy to take a hot bath and read a good book most nights, you're not going to need a closetful of evening dresses.

Clothing

Try not to shop on impulse and follow your master plan. Buy fewer clothes, but buy quality.

Fine. But what if you are even discouraged with the workmanship you are supposed to be getting when you buy a "quality garment"? What is considered quality these days, anyway? Whether we buy wearables at fashion boutiques or thrift stores, army surplus outfits or antique clothing shops, how do you tell if a piece of goods is really well made?

John Brennan, manager of the Brooks Brothers store in Cincinnati and Pat di Lonardo, their master tailor, spent much time helping me compile a list of clothing "should-haves."

Starting with a suit coat, put your hand in the shoulder and observe how the sleeve hangs. The underneath seam of the sleeve should never show and the sleeve itself should cover one-half of the pocket. If it doesn't, and if the underneath seam twists around to reveal itself, the sleeve has been improperly sewn into the shoulder.

Check the lining. Is the material compatible with the jacket material? If it's too heavy, it will hang unevenly and pull the fabric.

Living Better

Between the front of the jacket and the inside lining, a layer of canvas is sandwiched. Can you pull the jacket material and the lining material away from the canvas? If not, if the front of the jacket feels stiff, the canvas has been fused to the suit material, not sewn. Fusing means the two pieces have been glued together which is a common method of constructing garments these days. This is not to say it is not a good practice. Just know what you're getting. In dry cleaning, sometimes the glue comes loose from the canvas and bubbles in spots. Other parts of the jacket which may be fused are the bottom inside seam and lining in the pockets.

Check the stitching on the lapel. Is it even? Do the stitches pull? On good men's suit coats, stitches should be 1/16 of an inch long. Examine the seam on top of the sleevehead. Is it uniform and has it been pressed open? If it has, that's a sure sign of quality.

Do the stripes or checks or whatever pattern match at the seams? Check the shoulder pads. Are they constructed of layers of material sewn together or are they made of save-money foam, another common substitute these days?

Clothing

Look at the buttonholes. Are they clean or are strings left hanging? Turn the jacket inside out and examine the seams. Are they turned under, finished and hemmed? In good men's suits, the lining covers only the front and the top half of the back of the coat. This makes altering the garment easier as well as making the fine finishing apparent to the customer. Full jacket linings can cover a multitude of sins. On the other hand, custom tailored suits do sometimes have full linings. But if you can afford one of these, you've been through several fittings and know there won't be any surprises underneath the lining.

I have been wearing Brooks Brothers boys' jackets for years. They are roomy enough so I can layer shirts and sweaters under them, they are perfect with slacks, and for about $50 to $75 I get quality material, good workmanship as well as very durable clothing. But even Brooks Brothers doesn't spend as much time crafting boys' jackets as they do the men's versions. Since boys grow out of their clothing quickly, investing so much time in their construction would drive the cost of the garment to a level few mothers would pay for a season's wear. Some of the boys' jackets I've bought at Brooks have been fused in places. But then, so had the designer jacket I bought in the ladies' department in one of my favorite New York stores - for $175. I found that not only had my big-name jacket been fused together, the sleeves were crooked, the lining hung unevenly and, in general, it was terribly put together. It "looked" great and that's why I bought it. Not any more.

Sidestepping jackets for a minute, while you're in the boys' department of any store, check out their shirts. Some of mine from Brooks' boys' department have lasted eight years and cost half as much as the ones in the ladies depart ment. Same with Shetland sweaters, pajamas, robes belts and slacks. Boys' departments always yield sizable savings for ladies.

Back to examining clothing. In trousers—both men's and women's—the seams should be serged and pressed flat. To save money, often the seams are serged together and pressed to one side. This makes a lumpy line down the sides especially after you have them dry-cleaned. (Skirts, too.)

Vera Raupe, designer/seamstress, whose clientele bring her collections of the best known fashion names to alter, has seen all the cut-the-quality-corner tricks from the inside out. In fact, she spends a great deal of time putting the quality touches back

Clothing

into these garments besides making clothes for customers whose love affair with ready-to-wear has ended. Her advice? Look at the seams in everything you buy.

Many today are left completely raw.

At the very least, they should be pinked to prevent unraveling. And many times, seams are not even sewn with compatible thread. For instance, if cotton thread is used on polyester fabrics, it will break because it does not have the same elasticity. This is what causes gaping holes.

Hems? Where they were commonly finished with tape or seam binding and sewn gently, or carefully rolled on fine evening dresses, many today are simply top-stitched with the stitches showing on the right side of the dress. Designers say it's a stylish look. What it does is save time, and therefore money, for them. Are the hems even all the way around, or do they dip in back, front, or the sides?

Check the buttons, hooks, eyes, zippers. Zip the zipper and pull on it to make sure it doesn't come apart. Zip it down. You may never find it again. The zipper should also match the texture of the material. If it's too heavy for the cloth, especially if it runs down the back of your dress, it gives you a hunchback look.

Living Better

Buying polyester garments? Check the material for elasticity. If you pull on it and it stays pulled out, put the garment back on the rack.

Long-sleeved blouses? Make sure the sleeves are the same length. And when trying on slacks, look to see if one leg is longer than the other.

The ultimate in fine sewing is achieved when the garment is as beautifully finished on the inside as it is on the outside. That is pure optimism these days. In today's marketplace you will rarely find it. But in examining what you buy, try to come as close to the optimum as you can.

What if we women staged a ready-to-wear revolution? What if we said to department store sales clerks and buyers and owners, "That's a great skirt. If you finish the raggedy seams, I'll buy it." Don't just object to gaping seams and falling-off buttons which stores accept as a fact of life and will readily remedy. But insist on better quality for the dollars we shell out. Yes, we know labor costs are high, and we can sympathize with the plight of manufacturers. But what about our plight? Today, according to the fashion trade, a $100 dress is considered a moderately-priced garment. But $100 for most of us is not a moderate piece of our paycheck. For that bundle of green we expect something that will hold up through more than a few wearings. Be vocal about what you want, what you expect. If more of us do that, it has to make a difference.

In pure disgust and despair, many of us have sought alternatives. Sew-it-yourself is no longer a homemaker's hobby. It is a necessity. And non-sewers are coming up with some pretty imaginative alternatives.

Government Surplus

In-the-know campus kids have worn army surplus for years. Far from being clothes for coeds, only, explore how you can enrich your own wardrobe with high quality clothes at not-so-high prices. Uncle Sam is a hard bargainer, and when he contracts with a company to make garments, there's a list of specifications that go with the contract. You are going to be getting quality for the money you spend.

Green or khaki fatigues with lots of pockets are basic pants you can wear most anywhere. All the knockoffs you see in the stores will be twice the price and rarely as durable. A fatigue shirt with nice big pockets can be worn as is, stuffed into pants, or over turtlenecks as a jacket. U.S. Navy leather bomber jackets with mouton collars from WWII are still being worn and loved by participants, and copied by fashion designers and sold for fabulous sums. Originals are available in some surplus stores and their patina only improves with age.

Thirteen-button navy pants are as classic as their flat-knit sweater counterparts. The middies are great with jeans. Flight suits with all the zippers are go-everywhere coveralls. Paratrooper white denim hooded camouflage snow parkas will keep you warm as you sail or walk along the beach.

Below-the-knee navy captain's coats and shorter pea coats wear forever, and again, have classic enough lines to match many wardrobe variables. Pleated, peg-top, WWII Wave pants look like what's in the stores today at a fraction of today's price. Make a poncho from an olive green or gray army blanket. Sling a gas mask bag over your shoulder to use as a purse.

If you are lucky enough to be able to shop a store with surplus clothes from other countries, you'll find treasures such as white, oiled wool British submarine turtleneck sweaters, British

Clothing

divers' silk undersuits which look like long underwear and make fabulous pajamas, British officers' collarless shirts (WWII's answer to today's big-shirt look), French army leather map cases which make smart-looking purses or briefcases, French blue and white striped cotton jerseys, yards-long French Foreign Legion white wool mufflers which Legionnaires used to protect their faces from the sand in the desert and which you can use to dress up any coat.

The whole trick to wearing army surplus is how you mix and match what you buy with other things you own. You don't have to get yourself up as if you were going off to war. Wear fatigue pants pushed into boots with an oxford-cloth shirt, a Shetland sweater and a boy's tweed jacket. Eclectic good taste. Yours.

One thing to beware of in military surplus shopping is signs in stores advertising "army-style" clothing. This means they could be cheap copies of the originals. During WWII, it is improbable that clothes were made in Korea. And generally, armed service clothing is cut full for easy layering and ease of movement. If the shirt you try on is tapered besides being tight in the shoulders, it may be a fake. It's hard to tell, because even the government contract numbers printed in the garments are being copied by manufacturers.

JUST LIKE THE REAL THING: ARMY -STYLE- CLOTHES

Experts have a hard time telling the difference. It's strictly a buyer beware market. Your best bet is to shop reputable stores where you can trust what the owners tell you.

Antique Clothing

Thrift shop shopping is nothing new. People have been doing it for years. Lately though, thrift shop shoppers have become tonier. People who have never shopped anything less than the best boutiques have caught on to the fact that the quality clothes they are used to wearing belong to yesteryear. Because antique clothing is being snapped up by eager buyers, prices are beginning to reflect their popularity. Still, dollars spent will often yield better quality than contemporary clothes and some styles are so classic, so beautifully made, they are eternal.

I bought a brown cashmere 40's jacket with wide padded shoulders, a pinched-in waist, bound buttonholes and intricate hand stitching in an antique clothing store. Purchase price? Twelve dollars. I wear it everywhere with a beige silk blouse, a

Clothing

full camel-colored skirt and it's a good-looking suit. The trick again, with antique clothing, is to mix it with contemporaries.

Silk bedjackets paired with jeans can go to parties. Victorian tea dresses, intricate lacey wonders, are being snapped up as wedding dresses. Turn-of-the-century petticoats turn into long skirts for a fraction of today's "hostess skirt" price. Cashmere cardigans, pure silk shirts and pure wool anythings are treasures in today's synthetic market.

Two bobbin lace doilies threaded together with a grosgrain ribbon make an evening purse. Old piano shawls? Wear them. Victorian white nightgowns? Summer dresses. Lace-trimmed rayon or silk nightgowns? No, evening dresses.

When you buy antique clothing, examine it carefully. Anything with a lot of age is bound to have some imperfections. How many can you live with? Hold wool up to the light and search for moth holes. Some stains in cotton just won't come out. Lace, buttons and decorative parts of some pieces can be salvaged and used to patch others. Once you begin to make the rounds of antique clothing stores, you'll begin to get the hang of how to use and wear what you find. But every antique clothing aficionado has struck out one time or another. I wore a beautiful white cotton Victorian nightgown to bed and woke up looking like I'd lost a bout with the Boston Strangler. The material completely shredded as I turned over in my sleep. But, so many of my purchases are timeless prized possessions, I figure I'm way ahead of the game.

Thrift stores are in every city. The more messy and jumbled looking they are, the better the buys. Ones attached to fancy schools or charities can yield good clothing, but also higher prices. Become a regular customer at a thrift store. Make friends with the sales clerks; they may save special goodies for you if you tell them what you're looking for. Know the day the trucks bring fresh merchandise in and get there early. The dealers will.

Antique clothing stores are where some of the greatest treasures are but prices are going to be higher than at thrift shops. Some, in bigger cities, where the fad has escalated into frenzy, charge higher prices than low key places in smaller towns.

Again, shop around. Check out secondhand stores, flea markets, estate sales. This is where dealers get their things, anyway.

Clothing

To help you develop antique clothing knowhow, three books are listed below. They also offer excellent alteration, washing, dry-cleaning, and repair instructions.

<u>Cheap Chic</u>, Caterine Milinaire and Carol Troy, $5.95, Harmony Books

<u>The Yestermorrow Clothes Books</u>, Diana Funaro, $6.95, Chilton Book Co.

<u>Oldies But Goodies</u>, Donna Lawson, $6.95, Butterick

Dye It

To give new life to clothes you have semi-retired, or to build a wardrobe from simple tee shirts you can snap up anywhere, tie-dyeing is the answer. Ricki Chrusciel, tie-dye artist extraordinaire, offers these rainbow words of wisdom along with some easy-to-follow instructions.

Tie-dyeing is as simple as it sounds. You tightly band parts of a cloth, then dip the cloth in dye. The parts that are banded will resist the dye and make designs in the material. Just know that you cannot dye maroon material pink. But pink fabric can be dyed a darker color. Light to dark is one of the few rules.

Materials you'll need include a stove, a large pot (not Teflon), a large spoon for stirring and lifting, lots of rubber bands, stacks of newspapers to work on and to catch the splashes, Rit dye, either in powdered form or liquid, and rubber gloves. If you use liquid dye, you'll need empty squeeze bottles to hold it.

Natural fibers such as cotton, muslin, silk and wool dye best. Synthetics require special processes which will not be discussed here. (Check the library for how-to books.)

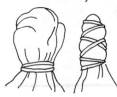

To form patterns, Ricki advocates starting with a simple one—the rosette. Pinch up a section of fabric and secure it tightly with a rubber band. Add more ties around the rosette to produce a sunburst effect.

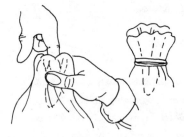

To make a donut, start out as if you were doing a rosette by pinching the fabric into a large puff, but then stuff the top of the puff down through the other side and tie tightly.

For diamonds, fold the fabric in half, then in quarters, and pleat the fabric from corner to corner. Tie with rubber bands.

Less orthodox techniques: Clip clothespins all over the fabric and see what happens. Tie popcorn kernels or marbles into the material. Secure a piece of fabric between two Tinker Toys with a C clamp for unexpected results.

Clothing

Standard procedures: Always wash and dry the fabric before dyeing to remove sizing and pre-shrink it. Work on a flat surface with wet fabric. Dissolve one package of powdered dye per yard of fabric into a pot of hot water large enough to allow easy movement of the fabric. Simmer for two-and-one-half to three hours until the dye is absorbed. The longer the dyebath, the richer the color. Then remove the fabric and squeeze out the excess dye. Rinse under cool water until the water runs clear. Drip dry and iron.

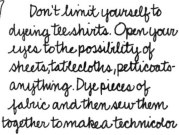

If you have followed this procedure carefully, your fabric will be colorfast and therefore machine washable with other fabrics. If you want to be especially careful, wash your tie-dye articles separately in cool water.

Don't limit yourself to dyeing tee shirts. Open your eyes to the possibility of sheets, tablecloths, petticoats—anything. Dye pieces of fabric and then sew them together to make a technicolor quilt. Make your own clothes from tie-dyed material. Ever think of using tea as a dyebath? Brew a pot of strong tea, add a teaspoon of salt or vinegar to set the color and add your material. Yellowed doilies or other aging material will take on warm grandma tones. A handful of onion skins in a quart of hot water with a pinch of salt or vinegar is another easy-to-concoct dyebath. There are dozens of natural possibilities in your kitchen and outside your door. Books that will tell you how to use them are at your library.

Finally, there is always a certain amount of surprise in tie-dyeing, so don't worry about doing it exactly the "right way." Expect the unexpected and enjoy the happy results.

Ricki Chrusciel's shopping and sizing hints:
"J.C. Penney's is a good place to buy 100% cotton tees. A size 14 girl's undershirt fits everyone from a size 14 girl to a size 38D lady. (Yep, it does.) Men's tee shirts work this way:

Men's small = Women's size 32-34
Men's medium = Women's size 34-36
Men's large = Women's size 36-38
Men's extra large = Wow! "

Getting it Together

A bandanna can be a scarf, a headband or a halter. A large piece of material can be a shawl or a sarong. A poncho pushed down to your waist can be a skirt. A long skirt pulled up over your bosoms can be

Clothing

a strapless dress. Old ties, sewn together, can make a skirt, too. Mechanics' overalls — your newest jumpsuit. Pare down and gear up. Ditch constricting ideas of what you think you're supposed to look like and enjoy making the most of what looks great on you—no matter where it comes from. Create your own couture, one dictated by how you feel and what you like rather than what the stores and the designers and the magazines tell you.

Low budget? Make up for it by tapping your rich imagination. You'll look terrific!

Look at it This Way

What you see is not what you get, it's what you make of it. Like using the bagels you bring home from the bakery as napkin rings at your next dinner party. They're helpful ice breakers especially when some of your guests are first-time acquaintances. Instead of using napkins, try bandannas. Use all red or blue or a combination of both. Get the big ones.

So many objects you pass daily can be put to surprising uses if you only look at them just a little differently. All the good things you find in junkyards and secondhand stores will be covered or rather uncovered in the Used and Abused chapter. This one deals strictly with what you stumble over daily.

For instance, if your toddler is a picky eater, whip out a muffin tin and put bits of food in each compartment and lunch becomes a game instead of a struggle. Use a lollipop as a tongue depressor if his throat is sore and you need to examine how red it is before you reach for the phone to call the doctor. Give him the lollipop as a reward. It will also soothe his throat.

If your kids have ever fallen and split their

Look at it This Way

lips, you know how impossible it is to get them to keep ice cubes wrapped in a towel pressed against the hurt for any length of time. Try a Popsicle instead.

If you're bringing flowers to a friend, keep them fresh in transit by sticking the stems in a balloon filled with a little water and secured with rubber bands. Leotards are fine bathing suits and cost about half as much as regular swimwear. (Other wearable alternatives are in the Clothing chapter.) If you're modest, stick to dark colors. They're less revealing when they get wet. Canvas feedbags from your nearest riding store turn into shopping carryalls. Some have handsome leather handles. They can also be used as planters and hung around the house.

Mexican serapes and Indian bedspreads are colorful, inexpensive tablecloths. Find them at any vaguely ethnic store or one that specializes in imports. Many department stores stock Indian bedspreads these days, too. Red clay flower pots bloom with spatulas, wisks, wooden spoons and all those other things you like to keep handy on kitchen counters. Wooden barrels, turned on their sides and appointed with a pallet filled with wood shavings can make a mighty snug dog house. Hang a piece of material over the door for added warmth in winter. Cut the barrel in half and you have two planters.

Living Better

Slip shower caps or plastic bowl covers over the bottom of hanging plants before you water them to catch the overflow and protect your floor. Sew buttons on children's clothes with dental floss or fishing line instead of thread in places where they get the most wear and tear. Slip a light bulb in the toe of socks to make darning easier. Glue corn pads to the rough bottoms of vases and art objects to keep them from scratching your tables. Vacuum your dog when he starts shedding in spring. You may need help (let's hope not a tetanus shot) when you do it the first time, but then he'll get used to it. Beats brushing out all those furry layers. Keep a blackboard eraser in the glove compartment of your car to wipe off steamy windows.

Hang a shoe bag near your baby's changing table to hold diaper pins and ointments you repeatedly reach for. I sent a shoe bag to my teenage daughter at camp to hang next to her bunk (she was on top) for books, her brush and comb, and hopefully, her retainer. Saved climbing up and down to get what she needed.

Use an ironing board as a bed tray table for someone who is sick. You can adjust the height for eating or even working puzzles.

Look at it This Way

Buy inexpensive, colorful paper Japanese kites to use as room decorations. Dangle long dragons from the ceiling. Arrange two or three more butterfly kites on a wall. Heart-shaped palm fans, hung in clusters, can decorate your walls, too.

The grand finale! If you want to add a shower to your bathroom, part of your equipment should include a Hula Hoop. Suspend it over your bathtub and you have a shower curtain rod.

Now it's your turn to play.

111

Shop at Home

Elbow to rib combat in department stores was never my favorite Christmas sport. And coming home from shopping forays in a flaming snit year after year finally convinced me to find a better way to buy presents for people I care about.

Avoid the whole scene—shop by mail. There are thousands of catalogues you can write for that offer everything from exotic plants to extraordinary handcrafts—from all over the world. Here is how to find them.

Many national magazines get very fat close to Christmas by picking up extra pages of advertising from mail order houses. Look through them to get ideas and send away for those catalogues that appeal to you. Many are free, while some charge a small price plus postage. Chances are that, once you make a purchase from one mail order house, you'll find yourself receiving many more catalogues. It is common for companies who do business by mail to rent lists of buyers from each other. You may request that they not rent your name to anyone.

Shop at Home

All the department stores where you are a charge customer send you Christmas, spring and special sale catalogues. You can shop the very same stores you always did, but without the hassle. You can also receive catalogues from department stores in other cities if you write and ask for them (there may be a charge). Tiffany's, Bloomingdale's, Neiman-Marcus and I. Magnin, to mention just a few of the merchant stars, can be your personal hunting grounds even if you live on the opposite end of the country.

Another new phenomenon is the dozens of catalogues of catalogues blooming in bookstores these days. The Whole Earth Catalog was probably the grand-daddy of most of them, and it's amazing what progeny that grand-daddy spawned. From books that contain hundreds of places where you can order auto parts by mail to those that are larders for every kind of food imaginable, you can buy virtually everything you need without having to leave home. After canvassing bookstores and libraries, I have compiled a list of those catalogues of catalogues which are most readily available. New ones, however, generally appear each season.

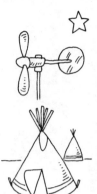

☆ The Whole Earth Catalog has vanished from bookstores (you can find it in libraries), but has been replaced by The Last Whole Earth Catalog ($6) and The Whole Earth Epilog ($4), both by Stewart Brand, published by Penguin Books. From how to buy reproduction furniture made in the Shaker Workshop to where to obtain books on parenthood, non-parenthood, Chinese medicine, and independent film-making, these books are the last word on where to get information on close-to-the-earth, alternative living.

☆ The Whole Kids Catalog ($5.95) and The Second Whole Kids Catalog ($7.50), both by Peter Cardozo, Bantam Books, are a wealth of resources for children on where to send for science and ecology kits, gardening, handcrafts, sports and folklore brochures, and so much more.

☆ The Teenage Catalog, Jonathan and Harriet Webster, $7.95, Quick Fox, contains send-away information on subjects ranging from the rights of students to bicycle repair and maintenance. In addition, there is abundant material on camping, handcrafts, job hunting and books to read.

☆ The Goodfellow Catalog of Wonderful Things, Christopher Weills, $7.95, Berkley Windhover, is a guide to fine and unusual handmade crafts available from artists and cooperative workshops throughout America. Just the pictures tucked inside these pages make this an exciting book.

Shop at Home

 ☆ The Shopper's Guide to Museum Stores, Shelley Hodupp, $6.95, Universe Books, lists art reproduction gift items available from museum shops throughout America.

 ☆ The Green Pages, Maggie Oster, $7.95, Ballantine Books, includes information on such subjects as the best gardening books and magazines, how to diagnose plant problems, indoor gardening courses, and where to buy exotic plants.

 ☆ The Complete Food Catalogue, José Wilson and Arthur Leaman, $6.95, Holt, Rinehart and Winston, lists hundreds of mail-order sources for food, equipment and gadgets from all over the world. Listings include high-quality houses like London's Fortnum and Mason, Fauchon in Paris, William-Sonoma of San Francisco, Paprikas Weiss in New York. It's hard to miss, ordering from places like these.

 ☆ The Cooks' Catalogue, edited by a large number of people including James Beard and Milton Glaser, $8.95, Avon, describes and illustrates over 4,000 kitchen utensils and lists sources where you may purchase them. Entries are classy and classic, and solid advice is offered about which equipment is proper to buy for the purpose intended.

 ☆ Mail Order Food Guide, Ann Tilson, Carol Hersh Weiss, $4.95, Simon and Schuster. Listings include where to buy bread, cheese, coffee, tea, nuts, soup, game, fruits and vegetables. Good descriptions, but

not as complete as <u>The Complete Food Catalogue</u>.

☆ <u>The International Cooks Catalogue</u>, James Beard, et al., $19.95, Random House, A critical selection of the best, the authentic in kitchen equipment. This book also contains recipes.

☆ <u>The Photography Catalogue</u>, Norman Snyder, $7.95, Harper and Row, lists and discusses workshops, schools, books, camera equipment and its merits.

☆ <u>The Whole House Catalog</u>, by the editors of <u>Consumer Guide</u>, $7.95, Simon and Schuster, discusses the best products and tools for projects around the house and lists where to buy them.

☆ <u>The First Complete Home Decorating Catalogue</u>, Wilson and Leamon, $5.95, Holt, Rinehart and Winston, contains 1001 mail order sources, ranging from where to get lighting fixtures and carpets to bedding and baskets, to help you decorate and furnish your home.

☆ <u>Whole Car Catalog</u>, by the editors of <u>Consumer Guide</u>, $7.95, Simon and Schuster, is a complete how-to-repair-your-own-auto book which also lists manufacturers from whom you can order parts.

☆ <u>Thrill Sports Catalog</u>, by the editors of <u>Consumer Guide</u>, $6.95, Publications International, describes the sports and the equipment needed for such activities as hang gliding, speedboating and soaring.

Shop at Home

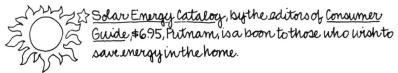 <u>Solar Energy Catalog</u>, by the editors of <u>Consumer Guide</u>, $6.95, Putnam, is a boon to those who wish to save energy in the home.

☆ <u>The Magic Catalogue</u>, William Doerflinger, $9.95, Dutton, lists tricks, their history, tells how to perform them, and gives sources to buy the equipment you need.

☆ <u>Cold Weather Catalog</u>, Robert Levine and Nancy Bruning, $7.95, Dolphin Books (Doubleday). This book says you can learn to love winter and shows you how by explaining winter games such as ice fishing, ice skating, ice hockey and snowshoeing. Other diversions such as winter photography and winter stargazing plus indoor activities such as candle-making, are also described. Mail-order suppliers are listed.

☆ <u>The Whole Baby Catalog</u>, Cathy Roberts Ross and Denise Marie Beggs, $6.95, Drake. Chapters deal with pregnancy, labor and delivery, toys and books, effective fathering, traveling with children and how working parents can cope. Organizations that deal with exceptional and handicapped children are listed, along with send-away-for-equipment and toy sources.

☆ <u>Cat Catalog</u>, Judy Fireman, $6.95, Workman Publishing Co. Besides the graphics which are worth the price of the book, this ultimate volume for cat lovers contains information on breeds, genetics, reproduction, housebreaking, geriatrics, how and what to feed besides listing cat clubs, magazines, humane organizations, and places to send for equipment.

National Directory of Addresses and Telephone Numbers, edited by Stanley R. Greenfield, $9.95, Bantam Books. Lists of selected addresses and phone numbers of government agencies, universities, foundations, hospitals, car rental systems, airlines, newspapers, TV stations – to name a few of the thousands included in this book.

The Catalogue of American Catalogues, $4.95, and The New Catalogue of Catalogues, $7.95, both by Maria De La Iglesias, Random House, have gone out of print, but are available at libraries. It's worth your while to look them up for the myriad sources they contain.

The Catalog of Free Things, Jeffrey Feinman and Mark Weiss, $6.95, Morrow. This book promises free things which turn out to be hundreds of how-to brochures you can obtain (free) from companies and government agencies.

The Catalog of Kits, Jeffrey Feinman, $6.95, Morrow. Send-away kits for making everything from pickles and clavichords to cars and kayaks.

The Jewish Catalog, $5.95, and The Second Jewish Catalog, $7.50, Richard Siegel, Sharon Strassfeld

Shop at Home

and Michael Strassfeld, Jewish Publication Society of America, have also vanished from bookstores, but surface in libraries. They discuss holidays, law, rituals and symbols as well as list addresses of Jewish movements, schools, organizations, magazines and kosher food sources.

The Jewish Yellow Pages, Mae Shafter Rockland with Michael Aaron Rockland, $7.95, Shocken Books, describes, with photos, where to buy crafts from Jewish artists, plus sources for food, antiques, learning programs and periodicals.

The Tennis Catalog, Moira Duggan, $7.95, Macmillan Rutledge, is a guide to all tennis equipment, from shoes to court maintenance machines. This book also lists schools and resorts by state.

The Travel Catalogue, Karen Cure, $6.95, Holt, describes myriad vacation spots and trips plus lists the contacts for making arrangements and obtaining information.

Whole Sex Catalogue, edited by Bernhardt J. Hurwood, $6.95, Pinnacle Books, gives resources and information on such subjects as sex and the law, sexuality projects, body awareness centers, therapists and techniques. The best-known bordellos are listed by state as well as a toll-free swingers' hotline.

Living Better

<u>Whole Health Catalogue</u>, Shirley Linde, $6.95, Rawson, deals with how to stay well cheaper. Hints on how to stop smoking to how to make the most out of visits to your doctor are given. A directory of national agencies on where to get aid for specific medical problems is included.

Although shopping by mail can simplify our lives, the process is not always foolproof. One headache is orders that arrive too late for the occasion for which they were intended. If merchandise does arrive late - later than the shipper promised - you don't have to accept the merchandise or pay for it either. Did you know that? As a mailorder shopper, you have specific rights and you should know what they are. Also, though most advertisers operate honest businesses, unfortunately there are hustlers in every field - even by mail. So, if you send away for something, never receive it and never get an answer from the company who supposedly shipped it, there are agencies who will help you get your money back.

The Federal Trade Commission says, by law, you have the right to know when you can expect merchandise to be shipped. If an ad says your merchandise will be rushed to you within a specific length of time, that is exactly what must happen. If no date is

Shop at Home

stated by the shipper, you have the right to have your merchandise shipped to you within 30 days. If neither of these rules is complied with, this is what you can do.

You have the right to cancel your order and get all your money back. If there is to be a delay in shipping, the seller must notify you of this and give you a free means to reply (for example, a postage-paid postcard). If you don't want the merchandise after you are notified of the delay, you still have the right to cancel the order and get your money back. You may also agree to the delay, or you have the right to not answer. But, if you don't respond, the seller will assume you agree to the delay. If the shipping delay is going to be more than 30 days, you must give your consent to this. Otherwise the seller must return your money at the end of the first 30-day delay.

You have the right to get all your money back if you cancel an order, and your refund should be mailed to you within seven business days after you cancel your purchase. Where there is a credit sale, the seller has one billing cycle to adjust your account.

If a mail order dealer does not comply with these rules, write to him and try to settle amicably. But if the situation gets nasty, call in the F.T.C. Either write Director, Bureau of Consumer Protection, Federal Trade Commission, Washington D.C. 20580 or call your Federal Information Center (see the Using the Feds chapter for your correct phone number) for the F.T.C. office in your area.

My experience is that the closer to you the agency is that you deal with, the faster the action is.

Whomever you write to, outline the facts of the case briefly and enclose copies of the advertisement you responded to, plus copies of all correspondence and any other related evidence.

The U.S. Postal Service also offers aid. If you believe you have been dishonestly dealt with, call your postmaster and briefly explain the case. He will either ask you to contact the postmaster of the city where the merchandise was shipped or do it for you. In either case, your complaint will be brought to the company's attention. But a postmaster does not have law enforcement authority. If there is still no action, the complaint will be turned over to a postal inspector, who has the power to cut off mail delivery, close post office boxes and prosecute violators.

For a great free booklet containing information on mail fraud laws, write to the Chief Postal Inspector, United States Postal Service, Washington, D.C. 20260.

One more word about ordering by mail. If you receive merchandise you did not order, federal law says you may consider it a gift and keep it without paying for it—no matter what the sender says to you or what he threatens. There are only two kinds of unordered merchandise which can be sent legally through the mail. One is free samples, plainly marked as such, or merchandise mailed by a charitable organization asking for contributions. You may also keep these items without obligation. So, if you are ever sent unordered merchandise and then hassled about it, contact the F.T.C.

Giving and Wrapping

A pox on pseudo old-fashioned coffee grinders filled with stale coffee that are hot sellers at Christmas. While it's oh, so easy to call a department store and order a "gift item" like that, have it wrapped, a card enclosed and sent out, why not buy a pound of the best coffee for someone who will appreciate it and tie the package with a ribbon? It conveys the thought better, more honestly and will probably save you money. Pre-packaged gifties are always more costly and usually of less quality than presents you put together yourself. You can still have the store send it out if that's a problem. The whole giving scene has gotten so commercial, rediscovering basics opens up a world lots of us have forgotten.

Christmas. Christmas Stockings.

Fill little kids' stockings with dimestore finds. The stationery counter yields dozens of possibilities — new pointy crayons, colored chalk and colored paper, bags of gold stars, Magic Markers, tablets, tape, glue — you can keep children occupied all winter long. You don't have to use these things only in stockings, you can make up your own "gift boxes" or fill a brown paper bag and tie it closed with a ribbon for any-time-of-year great gifts. Remember pickup sticks? Pick up a package of them and some jacks and a ball, magic soap bubbles and a wand, a jumprope, clay, Old Maid, a high-bouncing ball—got the idea? Scout a novelty store for squirt rings, plastic ice cubes with a fly inside, snapping gum, pencils with rubber points, vanishing ink, a can of nuts with a snake that pops out of it. Fill a stocking with football and baseball cards or lip gloss, shampoo, a pocket mirror, hair ribbons and headbands for a budding teenager. How about a stocking stuffed with chocolate-filled gold coins or bubble gum? A stocking stuffed with kitchen gadgets like measuring spoons, whisks, and spatulas may not be romantic, but it sure comes in handy. The same goes for assorted chisels, screw drivers, nails and hammers.

Make up a package of travel aids like collapsible drinking cups, toothbrushes and medicine vials for someone who is going on a trip. Fill a garbage can with dustpans, wisk brooms, can openers and all the things people need when they move into a new apartment or house. Notions departments, novelty stores, drugstores,

Giving and Wrapping

hardware stores yield endless doodads people need and almost never buy for themselves.

Instead of buying a box of note cards as a gift, make up a package of art reproduction post cards you can buy at a museum. Museum, zoo, and natural history museum gift shops are always good places to come up with treasures.

Bake a loaf of bread and wrap it with a jar of homemade preserves. If you don't have time to bake, any good fresh bread, along with some super-fine preserves you buy, will work as well. Fill a basket with apples or any kind of fruit and take it to a friend. Gather a rainbow selection of sherbet, tie the containers together and it's a perfect gift. Edibles always work well as gifts, especially if you can find an unusual item someone has an affinity for.

Gone With The Wind, The Little Engine That Could, War and Peace, The Secret Garden - a good book, a classic, is always welcome. Raggedy Ann, a teddy bear, a doll that does nothing except let you squeeze her. Cooking lessons, tap dance lessons, massages - arrange them.

Garage sale high-heeled shoes and sequin dresses and terrible old stoles, gaudy junk jewelry, narrow ties, shiny-seated suits become dress-up wardrobes

125

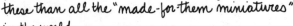

for little kids. What a present! A boxful of interesting jars, lids, spoons, strainers, sifters, scoops (again hit the garage sales and flea markets), salt boxes with spouts, spice tins, plastic containers for toddlers who would rather play with these than all the "made-for-them miniatures" in the world.

Have a photograph blown up to poster-size and give someone a homemade pinup. A Droste chocolate apple is perfect for the teacher. Fresh apple cider, a bag of popcorn and Monopoly packaged together (substitute a record if they're not the gamey type) can warm a winter evening. A wicker picnic hamper with a bottle of wine hidden inside, a salami disguised in an umbrella box....go on! You can do it! Just unleash your imagination instead of your wallet.

SEASON'S GREETINGS FROM UNICEF

Christmas cards. Consider buying them from agencies who will benefit from their sale. The American Diabetes Association, UNICEF, American Cancer Society, Arthritis Foundation, American Heart Association, Easter Seal Society are some who offer them. Check your local chapters or your favorite charity to see if you can buy cards from them. Tree ornaments. Think about making them. Cut out felt shapes and thread yarn through them. Make bread dough ornaments by dissolving

Giving and Wrapping

one cup of salt in one-and-one half cups of warm water and adding four cups of flour. Stir until the dough forms a ball. Knead until smooth. Either roll it out and cut out shapes with a cookie cutter or sculpt your own objects. Bake them on a cookie sheet in a 300° oven until they are hard. You musn't eat these creations, but you can paint them with Magic Markers or watercolors.

Easter. Give up giving bunnies and chicks that are often mistreated and soon forgotten. Instead, give a dog or cat from your local humane society a new lease on life – and a new home.

Valentine's Day. How about a donation to the Heart Association for someone you really care about? Buy a rose and tie a note to the stem telling what you've done. Pick up red heart balloons (novelty stores, again), blow them up and give someone special a bunch.

Mother's and Father's Day. Give promises – and keep them – like doing the grocery shopping for a month. Give a voucher for back rubs or for babysitting three Saturday nights in a row. Give someone breakfast in bed. Bake brownies. Cookies. They don't have to be perfection, just packed with good intentions. Don't forget to clean up the kitchen afterwards.

Birthdays, especially children's birthday parties, have become opulent affairs with pint size guests taking home party favors more expensive than the gifts they brought. Magicians and clowns keep the kiddies amused until they "play" games for prizes they kill each other for and go home angry if they don't "win." Here's an alternative—art birthday parties.

Cover your party table with shelf paper and put a balloon at each child's place. Have the children decorate their places at the table with Magic Markers and then eventually cover the whole cloth with designs. Provide white paper plates and let them decorate those, too. (Use non-toxic colorings.) Meanwhile have an undecorated frosted birthday cake ready in the kitchen along with a plate of big round sugar cookies and some jars of instant frosting. Have bowls of all kinds of candy—jelly beans, hearts, gumdrops, coins—in the wings, too. Let the birthday child decorate the cake with the candy while the guests frost and decorate their cookies. After everyone has eaten, remove the dishes and cover the shelf paper with newspaper. Give each child a paper bag with his name on it to hold four projects he will make to take home. They can be simple or more advanced according to the age of

Giving and Wrapping

the children. Some that are quick and easy are painting ceramic bathroom tiles to use as hot pads or coasters, stringing all kinds of beads (have bowls of them) on elastic string, making clothespin dolls (you need to provide yarn for hair, pipe cleaners for arms, maybe cloth scraps for clothes), painting walnuts to look like strawberries,

making mosaics from beans and corn, painting flower pots, making noodle wreaths - whatever you do easily and well. After the projects are finished, let the birthday child open his presents and then everyone goes home - happy. The key to success in this venture is superb organization. Keep the pace moving, have everything ready and get someone to help you. Bow out of the "big birthday" scene.

Wrapping

Wrapping paper can cost as much as the presents you put inside the packages and, since it is usually shredded so quickly, it's probably one of the poorest investments around. There are dozens of materials you can wrap with right under your nose that won't cost you a cent. Newspaper is usually over-abundant in everyone's house. If your daily newspaper has technicolor Sunday comics, save them to use as wrapping paper. Black and white comics work, too. Use the stock page, the front page, any page appropos to the person who is getting the gift or to the gift itself. Magazine covers or inside pages that relate to a person's interests are also fine. Brown paper bags resemble handsome craft paper when they are cut up and used to wrap gifts.

Or stick gifts inside the bag and tie it closed with jute or ribbon. Look through the glove compartment of your car for old road maps, search piano benches for sheet music and closets for wallpaper pieces and wrap with all of them. A woman I know says her

children are always careful with "first-time paper." All gift paper in her house is smoothed and reused for wrapping again. And again. Only thing you have to be careful of is not to give the person his own wrapping paper back on a return engagement.

You don't need ribbons either. Draw a dot-to-dot game on a child's gift so he has a game to play as well as a present inside. Paint a ribbon or anything else you can think of on the outside of a package. Let your kids do it, too. Blow up a balloon,

Giving and Wrapping

write the recipient's name on it and tie it to the package. Make a small bouquet of dried weeds you've collected, tie it with jute and tape it to the package. Glued-on dried leaves and pressed flowers are beautiful decorations. Tape a photo to the outside of the package – one that means something to the person opening the gift. Decorate the package with empty seed packets you've saved – they're beautiful. Cut leftover materials into strips with a pinking shears and use them for ribbon. If you must buy material, look for scraps on cut-rate counters wherever fabric is sold. Tie cookie cutters to the package. Or pine cones.

I like to give gifts in baskets so the person is, in effect, receiving two presents. It also eliminates paper and ribbons entirely. Wrap a baby gift in a receiving blanket or diaper. A teenager's gift can be tied in a bandanna. Same idea.

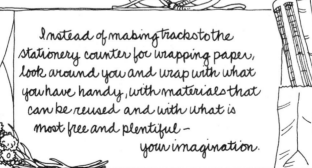

Instead of making tracks to the stationery counter for wrapping paper, look around you and wrap with what you have handy, with materials that can be reused and with what is most free and plentiful – your imagination.

Keys to the City

"Living in a city is like making love," says Bill Donaldson, veteran city manager of Scottsdale, Arizona and Tacoma, Washington and presently city manager of Cincinnati, Ohio." It's strictly a two-way relationship requiring work and understanding from both participants to make it pleasurable. And reading about it sure isn't a substitute for doing it." Wise words, I think.

Quality city living does take involvement and caring. It's easy to say the system is hopeless and walk away from it. But becoming involved, helping to shape policy, having a say in how things are done relieves feelings of helpless frustration. You are responsible for how your city operates. Or you should try to be.

A good place to learn how things work is at city government meetings. Find out when they meet and go to a few of them. They will reveal what the people who represent you really stand for. Chances are, if you're seen more than once, the officials will wonder why you are there unless you're vocally protesting some issue. (Politicians are suspicious!) Introduce yourself when the meeting is over. Get to know these politicians. If

Keys to the City

you need help from one of them later on, he'll remember you. It's effective.

Find out when public hearings are scheduled, and go to those where issues that concern you are being discussed. Some city governments have publications you can subscribe to, which list zoning change meetings, public works projects hearings and most of what is scheduled to occur in city government. If there is no such formal publication, call and ask what is on the Planning Commission's agenda.

If you are against an issue, express yourself. But do your homework and base your opinion on fact rather than hot feelings. Give the city officials intelligent reasons as a foundation for their decisions. People carrying protest signs who can't explain their position when they're asked have lost the point they're trying to make.

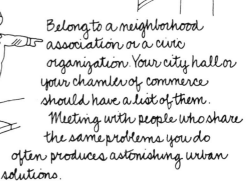

Belong to a neighborhood association or a civic organization. Your city hall or your chamber of commerce should have a list of them.

Meeting with people who share the same problems you do often produces astonishing urban solutions.

Living Better

To obtain information from a department in city hall, start with someone low enough on the totem pole who is charged with dealing with the public but with enough responsibility to help you. If you ask for the chief, chances are he'll pass you down the line and you may get lost in the shuffle. You can always work you way up the chain of command if you have to.

And don't start off yelling even if you are furious. Shouting is a sure turn-off, making the person on the other end of the line defensive and angry and probably unresponsive to what you want to get accomplished. Keep cool and say, "I have a problem. Could you please help me?" You may be connected to just the person who can solve your problem first time around.

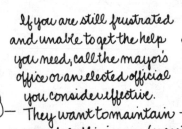

If you are still frustrated and unable to get the help you need, call the mayor's office or an elected official you consider effective. They want to maintain a good public image (especially close to elections) and their staffs are there not only to put you in touch with the person to solve your problem — they may even do it for you. Contact the one who has the most clout to get what you want done.

Keys to the City

If your city is small and doesn't have a full-time mayor or an especially active governing body, call the city clerk if you need help or information. He always knows everything that's going on.

City halls are also resources for information about your city. If you want copies of regulatory information such as building or health codes, it is available. Maps of the city, histories, neighborhood plans, pictures are on file, too. You may have to pay for some of these, but they do exist if you want them. Some city halls house a municipal library on the premises which is open to the public free of charge. They are great sources of urban information, especially if you or your children are working on a term paper for Government 101.

Urban Discards

You can buy used city equipment, usually by sealed bids, if you contact the city purchasing department and ask to be placed on their mailing list. You will then receive a bid application and be asked to identify what items you are interested in. Typical merchandise that becomes available is office equipment, fire hoses, scrap iron and broken water pipes. Most of these are sold in lots, but city vehicles, from automobiles to lawn mowers, may often be purchased singly. Terms are buy as is/where is with no guarantees..

135

Living Better

All the stolen goods recovered by the police department and sheriff's office that go unclaimed are auctioned off when the property room overflows. By law, a notice of the auction must appear in the newspapers well in advance of the sale. But to make sure you don't miss this event, call the sheriff's office or the police department and ask to speak to the officer in charge of the property room. He'll know when the next auction will be held and will also be able to give you a quick rundown on what to expect. There is always an abundance of bicycles, CB radios, cameras—just about anything that can be ripped off easily. Again, terms are buy as is, pay cash and if what you buy doesn't work when you get it home, it's yours anyway.

Unclaimed and abandoned automobiles—you know, the stripped-down doorless and wheelless jobs you see on the shoulders of the expressway—are auctioned off by the police department and sheriff's office, too. Many are not driveable, but are sources of spare parts if you're an automotive do-it-yourselfer. Can you imagine a broken-down car as a gift to a teenager itching to get his hands on a motor? Heaven. But then, you may luck out and get one that works. No guarantees at these auctions, for sure.

Post offices auction off undeliverable merchandise, defined as packages that are mailed and lose their labels in transit, damaged merchandise that the receiver will not accept which becomes the property of the post office, and merchandise that is refused by recipients and the sender does not want back. All of these items wind up at Dead Parcel Branches in 19 cities. When merchandise overflows, an auction is held.

Call the Claims and Inquiry Section of the main post office if you live near one of the cities listed on the next page and ask to be placed on their auction mailing list. You will then receive a catalogue in advance of the sale which will also state the rules of the auction. At most of them, merchandise is placed in canvas tubs and you have to buy the whole tubful. Be prepared for 50 wigs that didn't make it to a beauty shop or 150 8-track tapes sidetracked on the way to a music store. One-of-a-kind vacuum sweepers, typewriters and chain saws are not uncommon. The assortment

Living Better

is mind-boggling. Some auctions are two-day affairs. On the first day, you inspect the merchandise and take notes, because on the second day the bidding may be in a separate room. At others, all the action takes place in one day. The rules are buy as is and there are no guarantees. Watch the dealers in attendance. They know what they are doing. It's easy to get excited and overbid an item, winding up paying more for it at auction than you would retail. Take it easy. Even if you buy nothing, it's an experience to be there.

Dead Parcel Branches:

Atlanta, Georgia
Chicago, Illinois
Cincinnati, Ohio
Fort Worth, Texas
Denver, Colorado
St. Paul, Minnesota
Detroit, Michigan
Greensboro, No. Carolina
Jacksonville, Florida
St. Louis, Missouri

Los Angeles, California
Memphis, Tennessee
New York, New York
Philadelphia, Penn.
Pittsburgh, Pennsylvania
San Francisco, Calif.
Seattle, Washington
Boston, Massachusetts
Washington, D.C.

Other auctions, too good to miss, even though they have nothing to do with city surplus, are the classic car

Keys to the City

auctions put on by the Kruse Classic Auction Co. Representatives travel to cities from coast to coast holding auctions of Dusenbergs, Ferraris, 30's Rolls Royces, 1956 Thunderbirds - cars that are exciting to see even if you're not a serious buyer. If you have a car you want to sell, you can also contact this company for the participation rules. Write to Kruse Classic Auction Co., 300 South Union St., Auburn, Indiana 46706 for a schedule of their auctions, and hope that you live in or near a city on their itinerary.

Urban Homesteading

Urban homesteading transfers abandoned, unrepaired homes acquired by local governments through tax foreclosures and by the federal government through FHA mortgage foreclosures to people willing to take on the repair costs and be responsible for maintenance. Any citizen qualifies to take possession of a house (some are disposed of by lottery) for as little as $1 as long as he is financially able to pay for a rehabilitation job. In other words, you must have a steady income - how much varies from city to city. And you must agree to live in the house for a specific length of time. Most homes that come up for grabs - and people are waiting in line to do just that - are in viable neighborhoods that either show the first signs of blight or those that are rejuvenating. To qualify for urban homesteading and to learn the rules of the game, call your city's department of development or housing. Also ask about storesteading. It's beginning to happen in some cities, too.

Cities where Urban Homesteading is Happening—

New York, New York
Newark, New Jersey
Jersey City, N.J.
Plainfield, N.J.
Buffalo, N.Y.
Rochester, N.Y.
Freeport, N.Y.
Hempstead, N.Y.
Islip, New York
Nassau County, N.Y.
Chicago, Illinois
Joliet, Illinois
Rockford, Illinois
Springfield, Ill.

Gary, Indiana
South Bend, Ind.
Columbus, Ohio
Cincinnati, Ohio
Dayton, Ohio
Cleveland, Ohio
Toledo, Ohio
Dallas, Texas
Atlanta, Georgia
Decatur, Georgia
East St. Louis, Ill.

Phoenix, Arizona
Milwaukee, Wisconsin
Minneapolis/St. Paul, Minn.
Kansas City, Kansas
St. Louis, Missouri
Omaha, Nebraska
San Francisco, Calif.
Compton, California
Los Angeles, California
Oakland, California
Seattle, Washington
Tacoma, Washington
Philadelphia, Penn.
Indianapolis, Ind.
Baltimore, Maryland
Wilmington, Delaware
Boston, Massachusetts
Springfield, Massachusetts

Museums, Parks, Zoos

In the midst of urban sprawl, city parks offer us green respite. They also offer dozens of interesting programs such as nature study classes, bird walks, edible wild food classes, summer day camps and lectures given by park naturalists.

Natural history museums are alive with fossil and shell classes, bird identification workshops, field trips, lectures, planetarium presentations - that's just a sampling.

Zoos increasingly offer a variety of environmental education programs; maintain children's zoos where kids can "touch" animals; sponsor trips, movies and lectures.

Art museums offer art classes for adults and children, lectures and special exhibits. Kind curators will sometimes meet with people by appointment to help them determine whether their "treasure" really is one. Usually specific monetary appraisals are not given.

Zoos, art museums, parks and natural history museums commonly have volunteer associations which run gift shops and offer training programs for people interested in becoming tour guides. These facilities also make their libraries available for public use. By becoming a member of one of these institutions

141

you receive advance notice of all events, besides lending financial support to a worthwhile cause. Find out what goes on at these places in your city. For nominal costs or no cost, they are great enrichments to urban life.

Libraries and Theater

Libraries not only provide a wealth of reading material, but library staffers will also assist you in digging up information you need, whether you are involved in serious research or just require an answer to a simple question. If your library doesn't have a book you need, ask about inter-library loans. Your library can borrow books from other libraries within the state usually free-of-charge and out-of-state for a nominal fee. Libraries also sponsor lectures, films, storytelling hours for children; lend records and movies. Investigate.

Does your city have a resident live theater? Seats on preview nights (usually the two or three before opening night) are often sold for a few dollars. Ask about costume sales, too. When backstage wardrobes overflow, prop and clothing sales are held. Prime picking for Halloween gear.

Sports

Although professional sporting events are most exciting, you can watch practice sessions free. Call the home office of the team you are interested in and ask where it practices and when. It's a thrill for kids to see their heroes work out, and if they hang around until practice is over, they may come home with their favorite player's autograph. Players are more amenable and at ease at practices than at scheduled games. Check out college and high school team schedules, too.

Plant Tours

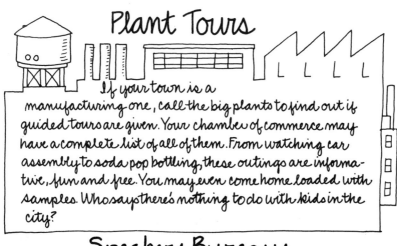

If your town is a manufacturing one, call the big plants to find out if guided tours are given. Your chamber of commerce may have a complete list of all of them. From watching car assembly to soda pop bottling, these outings are informative, fun and free. You may even come home loaded with samples. Who says there's nothing to do with kids in the city?

Speakers Bureaus

Turn the tables on the organizations that solicit your aid and ask ones like the Heart Association and The American

Living Better

Cancer Society if they have speakers bureaus that will provide interesting and free speakers for your club or group. Fire departments and police departments supply speakers, too. So do many athletic teams. And don't forget about city politicians eager for group exposure who will find it hard to keep your good will and turn you down at the same time. Call around the next time you need a speaker. You'll be surprised at the prize catches you can snag.

Use the Establishment

If you're new in town, your chamber of commerce can supply you with get-acquainted material about your community. If you're a long-time resident, but need to track down some information, your chamber is a good referral agency. Most have stacks of brochures about all facets of your city, keep a calendar of urban events and are eager to help you make the most of where you live.

The Bar Association, Medical Association and Dental Association are the groups to contact if you're unhappy with inappropriate billing or what you consider improper service from a lawyer, doctor or dentist. All have local review boards which investigate and mediate complaints.

Keys to the City

Local bar associations often have referral services manned by law students who recommend attorneys who will consult with clients for a small fee for the first hour. If you desire background information on an attorney, the Bar Association should be able to provide this, too.

Local dental associations and medical associations do not refer patients to a specific practitioner and never give medical advice. If you call and ask for a doctor or dentist to take care of a special problem, the association will give you a list of all the names in that particular specialty or those in your part of town. National medical and dental associations, however, have superb libraries of health brochures which you can write for - for little or no cost.

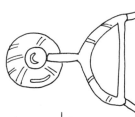

Write the American Medical Association, 535 North Dearborn St., Chicago, Illinois 60610 and ask for their free brochure, The Path to Good Health is Lined With AMA Publications, which lists all publications you can order.

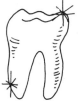

Write to the American Dental Association, 211 East Chicago Ave., Chicago, Illinois 60611 for booklets. State the topics you are interested in and a variety will be sent to you.

Schools

Universities and colleges are not only centers for educational opportunities, they also host movies, lectures, art exhibits and many other activities you can take advantage of. Call the specific department which offers subjects you are interested in and ask to be placed on the mailing list of upcoming events. A good number are free.

If your city has a college of music and theater, most probably there will be a resident symphony orchestra. Although professional symphony tickets are worth the price, taking your kids to a free performance of a college symphony orchestra is a good way to introduce them to classical music. If they get restless and want to leave at intermission, you're not furious at the money you've lost. Student recitals are usually free, too. These colleges also maintain concert bureaus, so if you're looking for performers to perk up a party — from jazz bands and chamber music quartets to ventriloquists and pop music vocalists — call and see who is available.

Architectural students can offer design ideas and draw up simple plans if you want to remodel your home or add an extra room. The cost of a professional to draw blueprints for a small job is often prohibitive. Call the dean of the architectural school and see if you can post a note on the bulletin board stating your needs. Students eager for experience (and extra dollars) will respond.

Colleges often sponsor low-price, almost-recent movies. Call the student information center and see if you can attend. Find out what else is happening that weekend, too. Need help of any kind? Call the student placement office and see if a student can do the job you have in mind. And don't forget about educational opportunities at colleges. New, adult, community education, short-term courses that deal with everything from transcendental meditation to belly-dancing are burgeoning everywhere. See if a class offered at your local college appeals to you. There is no end to what you can tap into at colleges and universities. Start making some calls.

High schools are increasingly attuned to vocational education which can be of direct benefit to you. Juniors and seniors participate in dozens of programs as varied as auto body repair and cosmetology to dry cleaning and printing. Students who repair auto bodies need ones to work on. Why not yours? All work is supervised by teachers. The price you pay is usually no more than ten percent over the cost of the materials. Compare that with professional prices and you will see how striking the difference is.

Living Better

Many schools have horticultural classes which run flower shops. You can not only buy flowers and plants from them at little cost, they will also do special arrangements for parties, even weddings. Some may also provide students to work in your yard. Gourmet food classes run restaurants which will cater. Bakery classes turn out bread and cakes. Air conditioning and heating classes may come to your home to fix your units.

Building classes, especially carpentry programs, can fill some pretty amazing orders. Graphics arts classes make signs while small appliance repair classes fix TV sets and radios you couldn't afford a professional to work on. The class offerings are as exciting for the students who participate in them as they can be for you.

To find out what vocational programs are available in your city, call your board of education and ask for a list of the ones offered at your local high schools. Or look in the phone book under your city's public school listing and call the high schools yourself. Ask if they have a vocational program. If they do, speak to the administrator in charge of vocational education and state the work you want done. He will put you in touch with the teacher of the program that can fill your needs. In the end, it is the teacher who decides whether his students are capable of performing the work which also must have teaching value for his class.

Barber and beauty school students also need customers to work on, although the schools do not advertise beauty service for fear of angry professional shops who resent the competition. Services range from permanents and color jobs to wash and sets and current cuts.

Dental schools have clinics where everything from orthodontia to oral surgery is performed. Dental hygiene courses are offered at many technical colleges as well as at dental schools. Besides cleaning your teeth, hygienists also take X-rays.

Taking advantage of what the schools in your city offer in the way of student services can go a long way to alleviate the pain of a pinching pocketbook.

City sleuthing yields untold opportunities. All you have to do is make creative use of what has always been right there in front of you — to your own best advantage.

Tripping

For travel information right in your own backyard, start with your state office of tourism. Generally located in the state capital, look in the phone directory under your state's listing for a general information number, call it and ask for the tourism number. Many tourism offices have both toll-free within-the-state and out-of-state numbers for your convenience. Or phone your nearest Federal Information Center to obtain the correct listing.

These offices offer a wealth of information on state parks, their accommodations, state festivals, even points of interest car travelers should stop to investigate. Many states have lists of farms which welcome vacationing families, make them feel at home overnight or longer and let children participate in the chores. Ask about Amish country, Indian reservations, lighthouses—the particular attractions the state you live in or wish to visit is known for—and take advantage of them to enrich your vacation plans.

Source Books

Two books you will find important aids in planning off-the-beaten-path vacations are <u>Country Vacations U.S.A.</u>, $3.95,

Tripping

and <u>Adventure Travel</u>, $5.95, both by Pat Dickerman. <u>Country Vacations</u> lists everything from seaport inns to dude ranches, while <u>Adventure Travel</u> covers how you can join bike, jeep or pack trips, go ballooning, soaring or rock climbing. These books are available at bookstores, or write to Adventure Guides, Inc., 36 E. 57 St., New York, N.Y. 10022. Enclose the price of the book plus 50¢ for postage. (In February, 1979, <u>Country Vacations</u> will be enlarged and the new price will be $5.95.)

<u>Country Inns and Back Roads</u>, the North American and European edition, both by Norman Simpson, $4.95, are personal accounts of homey, first-rate places to stay with detailed accounts of food, accommodations and nearby points of interest. These books are in bookstores, or write to Berkshire Traveller Press, Stockbridge, Mass., 01262.

<u>The Travel Catalogue</u>, Karen Cure, $6.95, Holt, Rinehart and Winston, is a complete source book for everything from assessing other vacation books to pointing out where you can find covered bridges. It is available at bookstores.

<u>Travellers Survival Kit Europe</u>, Roger Brown, $5.95, Writer's Digest Books, tells you what to do if you're injured or robbed, how to manage buses, customs officers, taxi drivers, money changes, even covers social behavior in each country. Available at book-

stores or from the publisher at 9933 Alliance Road, Cincinnati, Ohio 45242. Add 50¢ for postage and handling.

Also check bookstores for the dozens of Fodor's specialized travel guides and the Rand McNally guides including their <u>National Park Guide</u>, $5.95. Hundreds of other travel books appear seasonally. Take your pick.

Alternative Travel

Sharing car expenses with another person can really cut travel costs, but finding someone with matching plans is often difficult. People's TranShare is a good answer to this problem because it is a cross-country, non-profit transportation pool where you can register (for $15) to share rides with car, private plane, motor home or boat owners. There are walk-in registration centers in many major cities, or register by phone or mail. Whichever method you choose, your identification will be checked for the safety of everyone involved.

When you need a ride or want someone to ride with you, call the toll-free number and the operator will check the computer for names of people who are going your way. Then you contact these individuals to make definite arrangements.

Tripping

There are about 15,000 members of People's TranShare including 2,800 private plane owners. Call 800-547-0933 or write to People's TranShare Inc., P.O. Box 40303, Portland, Oregon 97240 for more information.

Another inexpensive way to travel is to register with an automobile or truck transporting company (listed as such in the Yellow Pages). You can drive someone else's car to an appointed destination (you pay the gas) by registering with the company. If you are the one who needs to have your car driven, you pay a fee based on individual state rates set by the Interstate Commerce Commission.

The largest company, with offices in 86 cities, is AAA-CON Auto Transport, Inc. Auto Driveaway is another large organization. Check your Yellow Pages for more.

Retired military can fly on military flights when space is available on a standby basis. A surcharge is applied according to how far you will be traveling. Spouses and children can travel, free of charge, on overseas flights only when accompanied by a member of the active or retired military.

Phone the Federal Information Center for the name of the military facility nearest you so you can see if you can hitch a free ride with your favorite Uncle.

If you plan to be in Europe for a month or longer and

Living Better

happen to need a new car at the same time, consider ordering a foreign car from a dealer in your city to be picked up overseas and shipped home when your trip is over. You will save the cost of renting a car to drive through Europe and probably pay a lower price for the car. Check with your dealer for the many import rules and be sure to make arrangements months in advance so the paperwork can be completed and car delivery can meet your travel schedule.

Train

A Eurailpass will entitle you to unlimited first class travel through fifteen countries in Continental Europe and the freedom to travel as you please. The cost is $180 for 15 days, $220 for 21 days, $270 for a month, $380 for two months and $450 for three months. A youth Eurailpass (you must be 26 or under) entitles you to unlimited second class rail travel for two months for $250.

For specific information, call a travel agent in your city. He will also be able to obtain a Eurailpass for you.

In the United States, consider a day trip on a historic steam locomotive excursion train. Children love them and it's a great way for families to explore yesteryear. A complete source of excursions is to be found in the <u>Steam Passenger Service Directory</u>. Write to them at the Empire State Railway Museum, Inc., P.O. Box 666, Middletown, New York 10940. The cost is $3 postpaid. Add 50¢ if you want the directory sent first class.

Major excursion operators you may also want to check with are Steam Excursions, Southern Railway System, c/o James A. Bistline, P.O. Box 1808, Washington, D.C. 20013 and Chessie Steam Specials, Passenger Department, Chessie System, 2 N. Charles St., Baltimore, Maryland 21201.

Water

If you are a canoe enthusiast, the United States Canoe Association offers members up-to-date canoeing news, racing schedules, information on techniques and more. Write to Jim Mack, U.S.C.A., 606 Ross St., Middletown, Ohio 45042 for complete membership information.

Grumman Boats, Marathon, N.Y. 13803 puts out the <u>Rent-a-Canoe Directory</u> listing over 900 canoe liveries in 46 states which you may write for and receive free of charge. Other booklets (also free) to request are the <u>Learn-to-Canoe Directory</u>, <u>Group Camping</u> by Canoe, and <u>The Grumman Book Rack</u>.

The American River Touring Association, 1016 Jackson St.,

Oakland, California 94607 is a non-profit, educational association offering professionally conducted raft trips as far ranging as the Colorado River in Arizona to the Suwannee River in the Okefenokee Swamp in Florida. Overseas trips including the Amazon River in Peru and Yugoslavia's Alps of the River Tara are included in their exciting schedule. For catalogues, dates of trips and fees, write to the above address.

If you're a houseboat fan, write for a copy of Quimby's Harbor Guide, Box 85, Prairie du Chien, Wisconsin 53821. It lists places to rent houseboats on the entire upper Mississippi River. Cost is $4.10 (3rd class mail) or $4.50 (1st class).

For luxury river travel with an old-time flavor, you can travel aboard the Mississippi Queen and Delta Queen steamboats along the entire Mississippi River. Meals, accommodations and entertainment are all first rate. For lists of ports where you can board, write to Delta Queen Steamboat Co., 511 Main St., Cincinnati, Ohio 45202 or see a local travel agent.

If you would like to travel to Europe by boat, but find the price of the Queen Elizabeth II too rich for you, consider boarding a freighter, many of which have fine accommodations.

Harian Publications, Dept. D, Greenlawn, Long Island,

Tripping

New York 11740 publishes two books which can help you make freighter arrangements. They are Travel Routes Around the World ($2) and Today's Outstanding Buys in Freighter Travel ($3.95). Add 35¢ for shipping and handling if you order from the publisher.

To charter a yacht, sailboat or for many other seafaring experiences, check the classified ads of Sea or Yachting magazine. Find them on the newsstand or write to Sea Magazine, 1499 Monrovia Ave., Newport Beach, California 92663 or Yachting, 50 W. 44 St., New York, N.Y. 10036.

Walk

The Appalachian Trail is a 2,000 mile footpath through scenic wilderness from Katahdin in Maine to Springer Mountain in Georgia. It's kept in its natural state for hikers only. If you plan trips for over one day, bring sleeping and cooking equipment you can carry on your back.

The Appalachian Trail Conference, the private, non-profit national organization which represents citizens' interest on the Appalachian Trail, publishes guidebooks and literature about the Trail and its facilities. To join and for additional information, write to Appalachian Trail Conference, P.O. Box 236, Harpers Ferry, West Virginia 25425.

If walking through cities is more to your taste, the Kinney Shoe Corporation has

157

prepared four regional <u>Walking Tours of America</u>: <u>Walking The West</u>, <u>Walking The South/Southwest</u>, <u>Walking The Midwest</u>, <u>Walking The East</u>. Each brochure contains maps, routes and describes points of interest to look for in specific cities. Brochures available through the end of 1978 - or longer, maybe, may be obtained by writing to Kinney Walking Tours, P.O. Box 5006, New York, N.Y. 10022. Enclose $1 for postage and handling for each brochure you order.

Wine

If wine is your pleasure, you can enjoy it by touring the many wineries found all over the United States. Three books will help you find them and tell you what to expect at each.

<u>Wine Country U.S.A. and Canada</u> is a small booklet ($2) containing listings and brief information you may obtain from the publisher, Reymont Associates, 29 Reymont Ave., Rye, N.Y. 10580.

<u>Winery Trails of the Pacific Northwest</u> by Tom Stockley, $2.49, may be obtained from the Writing Works, Inc., 7438 S.E. 40th St., Mercer Island, Washington 98040.

<u>Wines of the Midwest</u>, Ruth Ellen Church, $10, is found at bookstores or write to Swallow Press, Inc., 811 W. Junior Terrace, Chicago, Illinois 60613.

Go West!

If vacationing on a dude ranch sounds good to you, write to the Dude Ranch Association, P.O. Box 43,

Tripping

Granby, Colorado 80446 for their booklet describing accommodations throughout the western states. Then you can write the specific ranches you find most appealing.

An authentic covered wagon trip is an exciting way to see the country. Wait till you see the brochures! Two companies which specialize in these trips are Wagons West, Afton, Wyoming 83110 and Wagons Ho, 600 Main, Quinter, Kansas 67752.

To visit an Indian reservation, write to the American Indian Travel Commission, 10403 W. Colfax Ave., Suite 550, Lakewood, Colorado 80215 and ask for their brochure, Indian Country, U.S.A. listing Indian-owned and operated facilities.

The American Indian Calendar ($1), listing Indian events by state, may be obtained from the Supt. of Documents, U.S. Govt. Printing Office, Washington, D.C. 20402.

Wilderness/Wildlife Oriented Trips

If you are interested in wilderness trips, viewing wildlife, or just seeing natural beauty anyplace in the world, consider joining a museum or conservation group which sponsors these trips. Not only will you be supporting worthwhile institutions or causes with your membership fee, you will also be able to take advantage of travel opportunities

often led by outstanding profession-
als in the field. Check the natural history
museum or zoo in your city to see if they
sponsor trips, or consider these groups
listed below. They are only a sampling to
ignite your wandering spirit. Write to them
to inquire about membership fees and benefits (many include
subscriptions to glorious magazines) and trip information.

American Museum of Natural History
Central Park West at 79th St.
New York, N.Y. 10024

Smithsonian Institution
Smithonian Visitor Information
  and Associates' Reception Center
Great Hall, S.I. Building
Washington, D.C. 20560

National Audubon Society
950 Third Ave.
New York, New York 10022

Sierra Club
530 Bush St.
San Francisco, California 94108

National Wildlife Federation
1412 Sixteenth St., N.W.
Washington, D.C. 20036

American Wilderness Alliance
4260 East Evans Ave.
Denver, Colorado 80222

American Forestry Association
1319 Eighteenth St., N.W.
Washington, D.C. 20036

These commercial tour operators can be counted on to
provide professionally led exciting worldwide nature tours of the
finest quality:

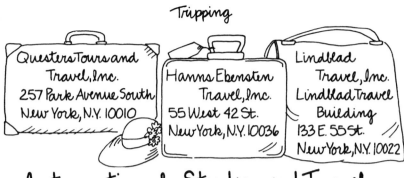

Questers Tours and
Travel, Inc.
257 Park Avenue South
New York, N.Y. 10010

Hanns Ebenstein
Travel, Inc.
55 West 42 St.
New York, N.Y. 10036

Lindblad
Travel, Inc.
Lindblad Travel
Building
133 E. 55 St.
New York, N.Y. 10022

International Study and Travel

There are many organizations which promote student exchange and travel. Here are a few interesting ones to give you an idea of the scope of those available.

The American Field Service fosters scholarship programs enabling high school students to live with a family in another culture (60 nations are involved) for a summer, semester or a year. For information on becoming a host family or how to qualify a student for travel, write to American Field Service International Scholarships, 313 E. 43 St., New York, New York 10017.

The Experiment in International Living, Brattleboro, Vermont 05301, sponsors semesters, summers and spring-breaks abroad for high school students, varied programs for college and graduate students plus exciting, broadening experiences for interested people of all ages. Write to them for information on their dozens of programs.

Study abroad for college students and graduate students is possible through programs administered by the Institute of International Education, 809 United Nations Plaza, New York, N.Y. 10017. Write to them for descriptive material.

The Council on International Educational Exchange, 777 United Nations Plaza, New York, N.Y. 10017, is a multi-faceted organization offering such an overpowering amount of benefits, any student who hopes to travel anywhere in the world should get in touch with them before doing anything else.

There are special discounts and benefits available from being the owner of an International Student Identity Card such as qualifying for student flights, check-in service at worldwide budget hotels, tours and so much more. Ask for their Student Travel Catalog (enclose 50¢ for postage and handling), the CIEE Flight Catalog and anything else new they may have brewing.

Earthwatch helps sponsor research expeditions as varied as those studying prehistoric man through excavation techniques on the island of Majorca, to observing the iguanas of the Galapagos Islands. They match people's interests with projects that need interested people along to share the work, costs and excitement of field research. Those who sign aboard help underwrite the cost of the project. It's a great travel study opportunity for anyone from 16 to 75 years of age—even entire families. Write to Earthwatch, 10 Juniper Rd., Box 127, Belmont, Mass. 02178 for more information.

Work/Travel

If you can combine work with travel, you've got it made. Here are four books that can help you land a job in an appealing part of the world. They can be found at bookstores or order from Writer's Digest Books, 9933 Alliance Rd., Cincinnati, Ohio 45242. Add 50¢ for each book for postage and handling.

Summer Jobs in Britain, $5.95
The Directory of Overseas Summer Jobs, $6.95
1979 Summer Employment Directory of
the United States, $7.95
Kibbutz Volunteer, $5.95

Accommodations

Swapping homes with someone in another part of the world can provide exciting and inexpensive accommodations. By joining the Vacation Exchange Club, which publishes a book every February and April listing thousands of homes offered for exchange, you will be aware of everything from villas in Sardinia to houses on Harvard Square. You pay a

membership fee to the club which entitles you to receive the books listing homes. Then it's up to you to make your own arrangements with other members. Write to Vacation Exchange Club, 350 Broadway, New York, N.Y. 10013.

American Youth Hostels not only operate hostels in this country, but also all over the world offering accommodations to hostel members for as little as $2.50 per night. This organization sponsors bicycling, wilderness, sailing and European trips as well as hundreds of activities at local hostel sites. Write to American Youth Hostels, Inc., Delaplane, Virginia 22025 for more information on all of this.

The "Bed Connection" is part of the myriad activities of the Council on International Educational Exchange. It is their New York Student Center offering a 24 hour, seven day a week telephone system (212-695-0291) providing students with room reservations

Tripping

when they call. The Hotel Empire, across from Lincoln Center is the main facility, but when it is full, other hotels are pressed into action. The cost runs anywhere from $21 for a single with a bath to $9.50 per person for a triple without a bath, per night. From June through September, it's a good idea to make reservations in advance. Write to New York Student Center, Hotel Empire, Broadway and 63rd St., New York, N.Y. 10023.

Other reasonably priced student centers are located in San Francisco, Los Angeles, Tokyo and Paris. Again, the Council on International Educational Exchange is the place to begin researching for accommodations when you begin to travel.

<u>Mort's Guide to Low Cost Vacations and Lodgings on College Campuses</u>, Jane and Mort Barish, $5, CMG Publishing Co., Inc., describes colleges and universities all over the United States and Canada that offer low cost lodgings to adults, families and groups—not just to students. Many campuses even include the use of their sports and recreational facilities. You can stay in the San Francisco Bay area for $4.50 per night or have accommodations near Disney World for $4. This book is certainly worth it's price. Find it at bookstores or write to the publishing company at P.O. Box 630, Princeton, New Jersey 08540.

<u>America on $8 to $16 a Night</u>, Bob and Ellen Christopher, $5.95 plus 50¢ for postage, P.O. Box 47, Milford, Connecticut 06460 lists 2,000 budget restaurants where you can

Living Better

get meals from $2 to $5 and 1,200 motels where you can stay for $8 to $13 a night for singles; $13 to $16 for doubles. Lists of toll-free reservation numbers are included. Many of the restaurants mentioned are of the fast-food variety which may not appeal to everyone, but the no-frills motels are clean and certainly a boon to car travelers since many of the major chains' prices have risen so drastically.

Traveling with animals can be a problem especially if you pull up to a motel exhausted from a day's driving to find you are not welcome because your companion happens to be a dog. Write to the Gaines Dog Research Center, 250 North St., White Plains, New York 10625 (enclose $1) and ask for a copy of _Touring with Towser_. It's a directory of hotels and motels in the U.S. and Canada where your animals (and you) are welcome.

Travel Aids

Many travelers who have medical problems such as allergies to medicine, diabetes and heart conditions join the Medic Alert Foundation. Lifetime membership ($10) entitles you to an emblem to be worn as a necklace or bracelet engraved with your problem; the association's phone number which can be called collect anywhere in

Tripping

the world any time of the day or night, and your membership number. If you become ill or involved in an accident and are separated from your wallet containing your identification and medical information, the person aiding you can call Medic Alert and obtain all your medical information which is kept on file along with the phone number of your personal physician.

For a membership application, write Medic Alert, Turlock, California 95380.

A membership in America Calling buys you peace of mind when you travel through Europe without a planned itinerary. By placing pre-arranged coded messages in the classified section of the _International Herald Tribune_, friends or family members at home are able to send you urgent messages anywhere the _Trib_ is found. By phoning America Calling operators before noon, messages can be telexed to Paris and appear in the _Trib_ some four-and-one-half hours later. Operators are on duty always.

A membership which costs $22.50 entitles you to a code book and how-to information, one free message and is good for three months from the date of departure.

Join America Calling by writing to them at 3 Hamburg Turnpike, Pompton Lakes, New Jersey. 07442, or call their toll-free number 800-631-8984.

Living Better

Using the Feds

The federal government provides tons of useful information as well as innumerable services. Getting to them quickly and easily is the challenge. In seeking information, it's common to get shuffled from person to person on the phone until you are finally connected to the "right person" in the "right department" only to find, after you have repeated your story for the dozenth time, that this department doesn't handle your particular problem after all. It's a real tooth grinder.

To keep your teeth intact and to get off the referral merry-go-round, call your nearest Federal Information Center. They are charged with putting citizens in touch with the proper people at the proper agencies, disseminating information, and in general are a highly efficient key to unlock the workings of the federal government. Whew!

There are 38 Federal Information Centers operating in metropolitan areas throughout the country, but residents of numerous other cities have toll-free telephone connection to an office near them. Even if you live in a city not serviced by a toll-free number, it's worth the price of a long-distance call (or letter) to get needed information without hassle.

Using the Feds

What kind of information? Anything. From simple directional requests like "Where do I get a passport, a tax form, medicare information" to more complex questions like "what is the current value of gold" and "I'm going to be traveling abroad and need to know the regulations about bringing a car back."

The primary purpose of the F.I.C. is to put you in touch with knowledgeable people so you can gather the information you need first hand. But as a not uncommon example of how far this agency will go to provide service, let me relate this story.

A gentleman called an F.I.C. office and said that as a result of an airplane accident, his wife had a fear of heights. She hyperventilated when she was in high places where oxygen becomes thin. They had to drive out west and were afraid their route would take them over mountains high enough to bring on an attack. He needed information on the altitudes of the roads they planned to take. Undaunted, the F.I.C. specialist called the right person at the Department of Transportation in Washington who dug up all the facts gathered when these highways were built. He not only knew how high the roads were, but also the oxygen content of the air at their highest points. The specialist called the man back, gave him all the information he needed and wished him a safe trip. What more could anyone ask?

Federal Information Centers —

ALABAMA
Birmingham
322-8591
Toll-free tieline to
Atlanta, Ga.
Mobile
438-1421
Toll-free tieline to
New Orleans, La.

ARIZONA
Phoenix
(602)261-3313
Federal Building
230 North First Ave.
85025
Tucson
622-1511
Toll-free tieline to
Phoenix.

ARKANSAS
Little Rock
378-6177
Toll-free tieline to
Memphis, Tenn.

CALIFORNIA
Los Angeles
(213)688-3800
Federal Building
300 N. Los Angeles St.
90012

Sacramento
(916)440-3344
Federal Building
and U.S. Courthouse
650 Capitol Mall
95814
San Diego
(714)293-6030
Federal Building
880 Front St.
92188

San Francisco
(415)556-6600
Federal Building
and U.S. Courthouse
450 Golden Gate Ave.
94102
San Jose
275-7422
Toll-free tieline to
San Francisco

COLORADO
Colorado Springs
471-9491
Toll-free tieline to
Denver
Denver
(303)837-3602
Federal Building
1961 Stout St.
80294
Pueblo
544-9523
Toll-free tieline to
Denver

CONNECTICUT
Hartford
527-2617
Toll-free tieline to
New York, N.Y.
New Haven
624-4720
Toll-free tieline to
New York, N.Y.

FLORIDA
Fort Lauderdale
522-8531
Toll-free tieline to
Miami
Jacksonville
354-4756
Toll-free tieline to
St. Petersburg
Miami
(305)350-4155
Federal Building
51 Southwest
First Ave.
33130
Orlando
422-1800
Toll-free tieline to
St. Petersburg
St. Petersburg
(813)893-3495
William C. Cramer
Federal Building
144 First Ave., South
33701
Tampa
229-7911
Toll-free tieline to
St. Petersburg
West Palm Beach
833-7566
Toll-free tieline to Miami

GEORGIA
Atlanta
(404)221-6891
Federal Building
275 Peachtree St., N.E.
30303

DISTRICT OF COLUMBIA
Washington
(202)755-8660
Seventh and D.
Sts., S.W.
Room 5716
20407

HAWAII
Honolulu
(808)546-8620
Federal Building
300 Ala Moana Blvd.
P.O. Box 50091
96850

ILLINOIS
Chicago
(312)353-4242
Everett McKinley
Dirksen Bldg.
219 S. Dearborn St.
60604

INDIANA
Indianapolis
(317)269-7373
Federal Building
575 N. Pennsylvania
46204

IOWA
Des Moines
284-4448
Toll-free tieline to
Omaha, Neb.

KANSAS
Topeka
295-2866
Toll-free tieline to
Kansas City, Mo
Wichita
263-6931
Toll-free tieline to
Kansas City, Mo

KENTUCKY
Louisville
(502)582-6261
Federal Building
600 Federal Place
40202

LOUISIANA
New Orleans
(504)589-6696
Federal Building
701 Loyola Ave.
Room 1210
70113

MARYLAND
Baltimore
(301)962-4980
Federal Building
31 Hopkins Plaza
21201

MASSACHUSETTS
Boston
(617)223-7121
JFK Federal Bldg.
Cambridge St.
Lobby, 1st Floor
02203

MICHIGAN
Detroit
(313)226-7016
McNamara Federal
Building
477 Michigan Ave.
48226

MINNESOTA
Minneapolis
(612)725-2073
Federal Building and
US Courthouse.
110 South Fourth St.
55401

MISSOURI
Kansas City
(816)374-2466
Federal Building
601 E. Twelfth St.
64106
St. Joseph
233-8206
Toll-free tieline to
Kansas City
St. Louis
(314)425-4106
Federal Building
1520 Market St.
63103

NEBRASKA
Omaha
(402)221-3353
Federal Building
US Post Office and
Courthouse
215 North 17th St.
68102

170

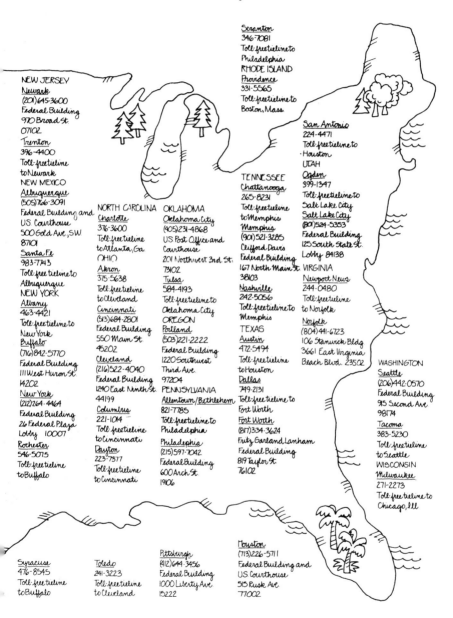

NEW JERSEY
Newark
(201) 645-3600
Federal Building
970 Broad St.
07102
Trenton
396-4400
Toll-free tieline
to Newark
NEW MEXICO
Albuquerque
(505) 766-3091
Federal Building and
U.S. Courthouse
500 Gold Ave., SW
87101
Santa Fe
983-7143
Toll-free tieline to
Albuquerque
NEW YORK
Albany
463-4421
Toll-free tieline to
New York
Buffalo
(716) 842-5770
Federal Building
111 West Huron St.
14202
New York
(212) 264-4464
Federal Building
26 Federal Plaza
Lobby 10007
Rochester
546-5075
Toll-free tieline
to Buffalo

NORTH CAROLINA
Charlotte
376-3600
Toll-free tieline
to Atlanta, Ga.
OHIO
Akron
375-5638
Toll-free tieline
to Cleveland
Cincinnati
(513) 684-2801
Federal Building
550 Main St.
45202
Cleveland
(216) 522-4040
Federal Building
1240 East Ninth St.
44199
Columbus
221-1014
Toll-free tieline
to Cincinnati
Dayton
223-7377
Toll-free tieline
to Cincinnati

OKLAHOMA
Oklahoma City
(405) 231-4868
US Post Office and
Courthouse
201 Northwest 3rd St.
73102
Tulsa
584-4193
Toll-free tieline to
Oklahoma City
OREGON
Portland
(503) 221-2222
Federal Building
1220 Southwest
Third Ave.
97204
PENNSYLVANIA
Allentown/Bethlehem
821-7785
Toll-free tieline to
Philadelphia
Philadelphia
(215) 597-7042
Federal Building
600 Arch St.
19106

Scranton
346-7081
Toll-free tieline to
Philadelphia
RHODE ISLAND
Providence
331-5565
Toll-free tieline to
Boston, Mass.

TENNESSEE
Chattanooga
265-8231
Toll-free tieline
to Memphis
Memphis
(901) 521-3285
Clifford Davis
Federal Building
167 North Main St.
38103
Nashville
242-5056
Toll-free tieline to
Memphis
TEXAS
Austin
472-5494
Toll-free tieline
to Houston
Dallas
749-2131
Toll-free tieline to
Fort Worth
Fort Worth
(817) 334-3624
Fritz Garland Lanham
Federal Building
819 Taylor St.
76102

San Antonio
224-4471
Toll-free tieline to
Houston
UTAH
Ogden
399-1347
Toll-free tieline to
Salt Lake City
Salt Lake City
(801) 524-5353
Federal Building
125 South State St.
Lobby 84138
VIRGINIA
Newport News
244-0480
Toll-free tieline
to Norfolk
Norfolk
(804) 441-6723
106 Stanwick Bldg.
3661 East Virginia
Beach Blvd. 23502

WASHINGTON
Seattle
(206) 442-0570
Federal Building
915 Second Ave.
98174
Tacoma
383-5230
Toll-free tieline
to Seattle
WISCONSIN
Milwaukee
271-2273
Toll-free tieline to
Chicago, Ill.

Syracuse
476-8545
Toll-free tieline
to Buffalo

Toledo
241-3223
Toll-free tieline
to Cleveland

Pittsburgh
(412) 644-3456
Federal Building
1000 Liberty Ave.
15222

Houston
(713) 226-5711
Federal Building and
US Courthouse
515 Rusk Ave.
77002

Living Better

Congressmen Are Useful, Too

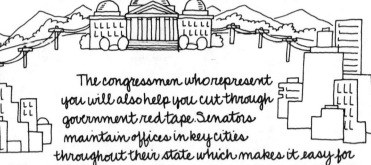

The congressmen who represent you will also help you cut through government red tape. Senators maintain offices in key cities throughout their state which makes it easy for you to call if you live in one of them. If you don't, phone the office in the largest city near you, state your name, briefly tell the staff person what you need and ask to be called back. You will be. All offices are hooked up to a federal telephone system which enables staff to call long distance anywhere without charge. Since U.S. Representatives are elected by district, reaching their local office is no problem. There will always be one near you.

The main thing to remember in dealing with elected officials is that you are the person who elects them. They want to keep a good public image and will go to great lengths to aid constituents. They are excellent facilitators. If your social security check is fouled up or medicare payments aren't coming through, the staff of these offices will investigate and find out what is holding them up. If you have written to a federal official and not received an answer, call your representative or senator. They definitely get answers. If you want to know the status of a pending bill, the

Using the Feds

staff of these offices will call Washington, find out and call you back. For information on already passed bills, they will call either the congressional or senate library and have a copy sent to you. In fact, they can get you copies of any legislation. You can also ask for issue briefs. These will give you the legislative history of what you want to know. Even analyses of pieces of legislation or issues are available.

If you are planning a sight-seeing trip to Washington, call your senator or representative's office first. They are able to arrange V.I.P. tour passes of the White House, Capitol, F.B.I., Pentagon and Kennedy Center. These are the same tours the general public takes only you won't have to stand in line. But each official is given a limited number of these passes per week, so call at least a month in advance (farther in advance for spring and summer tours) to reserve them. Then, once you are in Washington, stop in at your senator or representative's office to pick up a pass to watch legislative sessions in the House of Representatives and the Senate. They are enlightening to say the least.

Senators and representatives make appointments to military academies. If you are interested, call in the fall for an application for a spot the next year. Congressional offices also employ interns. Regulations differ but in some cases you must be enrolled in a college, university or an institution of higher education for an academic year previous to internship or you must be a bona-fide teacher in government or social studies at a secondary or post-secondary school during the year immediately preceding internship. Some positions pay. Others are voluntary. Either way it's a great experience. If you're interested, call your senator or representative and find out how you qualify.

Finally, congressmen can get you flags. Everyday American flags, or ones that have actually flown over the capitol. (These cost more.) And, if you live to be 100, you'll get salutations from your senator and a card from the president. Wow!

Extension Services

There are Cooperative Extension Services in every county of every state. Joint operations of the Department of Agriculture, state and local governments, each is associated with a state land grant college. What can they do for you? Supply you with free information, consulting services and written material on subjects related to anything that grows, home economics and 4-H clubs.

County agents can tell you what grass to plant where. They will accept soil and plant specimens which they analyze for problems or will send samples away to the college they are associated with for testing. Canning, preserve-making, nutrition information is supplied by home economists. From dressmaking to refinishing furniture, your questions can be answered. I called when one of my children left the freezer door open overnight to find out whether I could refreeze the food, or whether I had to cook it. I cooked.

The services are myriad, so take advantage of them. Look in your phone book under U.S. Government. The extension service will be listed under the Department of Agriculture.

Soil and Water Conservation Offices are located in each densely populated county or one may serve two or three less populated counties. Their primary concern is with soil and water erosion problems. If your pond doesn't drain right or the hill in your backyard is sliding away, an agent will visit you, draw up plans and help you oversee work to correct the problem. They also have hundreds of conservation pamphlets at their disposal, some much like the ones the county agent dispenses. These agencies do overlap somewhat. But one unique thing Soil and Water Conservation Offices offer is trees for sale. A mixture of fifty hardwoods, evergreens and shrubs costs $50. If you are involved in reforestation (weekend farm?), you can buy a minimum of 500 trees for $14, but they cannot be used for ornamental purposes as the others can. Call your district office to see if they have trees for sale. To find the office in your area, again, look for the Department of Agriculture subheading under the U.S. Government listing in your phone book.

Government Surplus

The United States government is one of the greatest sources of secondhand goods in the world. Since it supplies the equipment for people, hospitals, offices and wars all over the world, the range of merchandise for sale is vast. From paper shredders to airplane propellers, it's all available.

The Department of Defense is one of the biggest sections of the government department store. To buy from them, write a letter to Defense Surplus Sales, P.O. Box 1370, Battle Creek, Michigan 49016 stating that you would like to bid on surplus property. You will receive an application which states the categories of goods available. (Textiles, office equipment, etc.) Also on the form, there will be places for you to check the states in which you want to receive notices of auctions. When you return the application, you will then be placed on the National Bidders List and will receive catalogues of items coming up for auction in advance of the sales. Most are purchased by sealed bids which you mail in. If you participate in auctions, you will remain on the mailing list. If you don't, after you have received five catalogues, your name will be dropped. So, when you check states and categories on the application, don't overextend yourself or you'll continually have to reapply.

On-the-site auctions at military facilities are common also. To be aware of these, write to the same address and ask to be placed on the bidders list for sales in your area. State just how far-reaching an area you are willing to travel to attend them. When you receive the application, again check the classifications you are interested in, mail it back and you will be placed on the mailing list and will begin receiving catalogues.

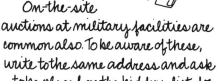

Rules are : everything is bought as is/where is. If you buy a jeep by sealed bid 300 miles away, you're going to have to go get it and bring it home, no matter what shape it's in. Also remember, if its feasible for the government to

177

have fixed it, they would have. If it has gone up for bids, it needed more repair than maybe it is worth. It's strictly a take-your-chances market.

There are also retail stores at 40 military facilities throughout the country run by the Defense Property Disposal Service. The stock varies according to the facility that houses the store and hours are irregular. Write to Federal Center, D.P.D.S.-M.M.S., Battle Creek, Michigan 49016 and ask for the military retail store nearest you. Then, you'll have to call or write the facility for shopping hours.

The General Services Administration is also a huge source of secondhand goods which they dispose of by auction. Write in care of Sales, General Services Administration, Federal Supply Service to the one nearest you (see list below) for a bid application. The procedure is generally the same as for Department of Defense sealed bid auctions. Cars are a frequent item as is office and hospital equipment.

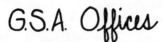

G.S.A. Offices

832 Post Office Building
Boston, Massachusetts 02109
(for Connecticut, Maine, Massachusetts, New Hampshire,

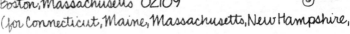

Rhode Island, Vermont)

26 Federal Plaza
New York, New York 10007
(for New Jersey, New York, Puerto Rico, Virgin Islands)

7th and D Streets SW
Washington, D.C. 20407
(for Delaware, District of Columbia, Maryland, Pennsylvania,
Virginia, West Virginia)

1776 Peachtree St., NW
Atlanta, Georgia 30309
(for Alabama, Florida, Georgia, Kentucky, Mississippi, North
Carolina, South Carolina, Tennessee)

230 South Dearborn St.
Chicago, Illinois 60604
(for Illinois, Indiana, Michigan, Minnesota, Ohio, Wisconsin)

1500 East Bannister Rd.
Kansas City, Missouri 64131
(for Iowa, Kansas, Missouri, Nebraska)

819 Taylor St.
Fort Worth, Texas 76102
(for Arkansas, Louisiana, New Mexico, Oklahoma, Texas)

Denver Federal Center, Building 41
Denver, Colorado 80225
(for Colorado, Montana, North Dakota, South Dakota, Utah, Wyoming)

Living Better

525 Market St.
San Francisco, California 94105
(for Arizona, California, Nevada)

GSA Center
915 Second Ave.
Seattle, Washington 98104
(for Idaho, Oregon, Washington)

Post Office
Courthouse and Customhouse
335 South King St.
Honolulu, Hawaii 96813
(Hawaii Area)

Post Office Box 160
Anchorage, Alaska
99501
(Alaskan Area)

The U.S. Customs Service also auctions off unclaimed merchandise. The best and most frequent auctions occur in gateway cities where import traffic is heaviest. But other cities also accumulate merchandise over longer periods of time, so call the office in your city to see if and when they hold auctions. You can also ask to be placed on their auction mailing list so you will know about them in advance. Look in the phone book for the U.S. Government listing. The Customs Service will be under the Treasury Department subhead.

The Internal Revenue Service auctions off seized property of people who couldn't come up with the cash to pay Uncle Sam. Furs, jewelry—anything of value is likely to turn up.

Using the Feds

Call the office in your city to see if auctions are held (they may be in your city or one close to you in your district) and ask to be placed on the mailing list to receive advance notices. Some property is disposed of by sealed bid auctions. Some are held on the site.

The Department of Housing and Urban Development also attaches property, and repossessed homes may be auctioned off. A number of federal departments are involved in this disposal, so to reach just the right person in the agency in charge, call your Federal Information Center.

Government Publications

Each year the departments, offices and agencies of the federal government print tens of thousands of publications. From small pamphlets to multi-volume reports, some are free and some are for sale. Subjects range anywhere from how to recognize poison ivy to how to get better gas mileage.

A key to finding the ones you want is a small pamphlet (free) you can send for from the U.S. Government Printing Office, Superintendent of Documents, Washington, D.C. 20402 entitled <u>Consumers Guide to Federal Publications</u>. In it, all government publications have been grouped into bibliographies by subject. Send for it, check the bibliographies you want on the order form and mail it back to the same address. The bibliographies will be mailed to you. Then you can choose what individual brochures you want—and then—mail your order off again. The only problem with all this is the turtle speed of this office in filling orders. Although they say they are trying to do better, response time still takes four to six weeks. Sometimes longer.

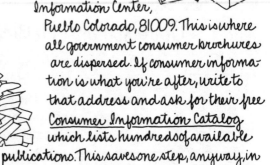

Another mailing address commonly seen in publications is the Consumer Information Center, Pueblo Colorado, 81009. This is where all government consumer brochures are dispersed. If consumer information is what you're after, write to that address and ask for their free <u>Consumer Information Catalog</u> which lists hundreds of available publications. This saves one step, anyway, in the back and forth mailathon to Washington.

If you live in a city (there are 20), where the Government Printing Office maintains a bookstore, you can bypass all these postal procedures. Call your Federal Information Center and ask for the one nearest you. If conveniently located, you may want to stop in personally and buy your selected pamphlets on the spot.